Deeply rooted in Scripture and practica
ment in a multicultural church in South
magnificently. He spells out his thoroughgoing yet patient commitment
to the biblical ideal of enthusiastically embracing diversity in the local
church, to the glory of God.

Terry Virgo (Newfrontiers)

Crossing the Divide is a straight-on look at both the challenges and the
blessings of diversity within the body of Christ. Owen Hylton simplifies
and clarifies the complexity of such a dicey topic, all for and to the glory
of God.

Dr David Anderson
Senior Pastor, Bridgeway Community Church, Columbia, MD, USA,
and author of Gracism

Open, real and challenging, full of theological, pastoral and leadership
insight, and a must-read for anyone involved in a local church which is
growing in diversity.

Steve Tibbert
Senior Pastor, King's Church, Catford

Rooted in biblical truth and gathered from the experiences of a pastor
who is intentional about building a multicultural church, this book dis-
plays a practical outworking of God's own passion to gather for himself a
people from all the nations.

Gavin Peacock
Former Chelsea captain and Match of the Day commentator,
currrently studying theology in preparation for church ministry

Crossing the
the
Divide

Owen Hylton

Crossing
the
Divide

A call to embrace diversity

ivp

INTER-VARSITY PRESS
Norton Street, Nottingham NG7 3HR, England
Email: ivp@ivpbooks.com
Website: www.ivpbooks.com

First published 2009

British Library Cataloguing in Publication Data
A catalogue record for this book is available from the British Library.

ISBN: 978-1-84474-383-4

Set in Monotype Dante 12/15pt
Typeset in Great Britain by Servis Filmsetting Ltd, Stockport, Cheshire
Printed and bound by Ashford Colour Press Ltd, Gosport, Hampshire

Inter-Varsity Press publishes Christian books that are true to the Bible and that communicate the gospel, develop discipleship and strengthen the church for its mission in the world.

Inter-Varsity Press is closely linked with the Universities and Colleges Christian Fellowship, a student movement connecting Christian Unions in universities and colleges throughout Great Britain, and a member movement of the International Fellowship of Evangelical Students.
Website: www.uccf.org.uk

Dedication

To my girls:
Yasmin, Rhianna and Daisy

*God did not bring black and white together to make grey,
but a myriad of colours.*

Love you,
Dad

CONTENTS

ACKNOWLEDGMENTS

Writing this book has been both a releasing and a humbling experience for me. It was releasing because I have had a desire for the last five or six years to write on the subject of diversity in the church. I feel very much that God gave me something to say and then provided the opportunity for me to say it. It is also humbling because, while I felt I had something to say on this issue, I also needed help to be able to say it in a way that would hopefully prove meaningful and helpful. For that help I have numerous people to thank: some professionals, but mostly friends who have gone way beyond what one should really ask of them. To them I am deeply grateful for all the support, rewriting, structuring, biblical analysis, insightful comments and general encouragement. I would specifically like to thank the following people:

Phil Hopgood, a friend of thirty years, who went way beyond the call of friendship to read, comment on and give numerous suggestions to improve the text. Rosie Gillard, who provided much-needed help on the structure, referencing and headings and made many valuable suggestions.

Nicholas Ferguson, Martin Alley, Ted and Karen Hans, who all read, commented on and made helpful suggestions to the text, all of which has added to the quality of this book. Ted's support on the biblical analysis was particularly helpful.

Our friends Ron and Audrey Hopgood and my in-laws

Michael and Muriel Anns, who all provided places for me to write and constant refreshments!

Steve Tibbert and the other elders at King's Church in Catford, who allowed me the time to write and also lived much of this not-so-easy journey with me. I will always be grateful for your patience.

All the fantastic people at King's Church, many of whom are beginning to live this dream. Mary Lindsay, my former administrative assistant, who helped to collate all the journals, diary entries and testimonies, and, at what seemed like a moment's notice, helped prepare my original proposal.

Further thanks must also go to the following people: Jeff Crosby, IVP USA, who first took an interest in my idea when I spoke to him while on a trip to the USA and who later introduced me to my editor at IVP UK, Dr David Anderson, and to Joel Edwards, both of whom have been true inspirations and have offered much encouragement.

Thanks also to my editor, Eleanor Trotter, who has been a constant source of encouragement, giving wise advice and skilfully guiding me, a novice, through the whole writing process. Also, to all the people connected to IVP who have read and commented on the manuscript, I am most grateful.

Finally, my deepest thanks and love go to my wife Pauline, the other half of me, for her sense of fun, which helped me to keep going during low writing days. She has helped to shape many of the stories, illustrations and ideas in this book.

If I have missed anyone out, please forgive me. God knows how grateful I am for all the help I have received.

Owen Hylton
March 2009

FOREWORD

As a black Christian leader turned loose in a largely white evangelical world over twenty years ago I actually grew accustomed to being the only black person in public gatherings. If I'm honest, I was quietly smug about being the centre of attention as I showed up for a conference in some rural setting, or walked down the High Street in Belfast when I visited colleagues in Northern Ireland. Twenty years ago I could be a specialist in cross-cultural ministry simply by showing up!

Much of my work in those early years as the General Secretary of the African and Caribbean Evangelical Alliance was concerned with weaving relationships between African and Caribbean Christians in Britain, but I was also preoccupied with providing a bridge between black and white Christians across the church landscape. It wasn't all hard work: some encounters between our cultures included nothing more complicated than getting people to eat, talk and pray together. But it was also quite demanding, as we sought to strip away caricatures and mutual ignorance, or tackle racist attitudes in Christian institutions.

My appointment in 1997 as the first black General Director of the Evangelical Alliance in its 150-year history was important – but not only for me and black Christian faith in Britain; it was also a courageous step for the organization. As I explained in one of my first interviews, it was a vote of confidence for diversity. And over the twelve years I had the privilege of serving the Evangelical Alliance, the landscape changed dramatically. Thankfully, I became surrounded by other players and voices drawing attention to the need for racial harmony and diversity across our cultural streams. And some of them were doing it much better than I was.

But not enough of them have taken the time to examine the issues and help us through the challenges and joys of diversity. *Crossing the Divide* is an important contribution in this regard.

This book could not have been written a decade ago; it's a time and motion study in diversity in the here and now.

Owen Hylton isn't guessing about the issues he raises in this book. His biblical reflections and references are complemented by an accessible style. In order to weave a tapestry of experiences and insights to help us on our journey, he has trawled through real-life stories from friends, associates, fellow ministers and family members. But he has also taken us into his own heart and life, in order to provide us with some authentic and practical steps to follow.

There are very good reasons to cross the divide on race. In a world splintered with multiple identities and cultural conflicts, the church has an obligation to offer something different to those who come and walk with us in order to meet with Christ. But we also have to offer a biblical grammar with which to talk about a diversity that is rooted in real lives and which builds models of community cohesion that others might want to emulate.

As far as grammar goes, *Crossing the Divide* speaks eloquently to us.

Joel Edwards
Micah Challenge International
March 2009

INTRODUCTION

This journey unfolds on three levels. The first level is what we have been experiencing at King's Church in Catford, south east London, England. King's is a growing, diverse church of around a thousand regular attendees, a member of the Evangelical Alliance and also of Newfrontiers, a family of over 200 churches in the UK and over 500 around the world. (At the time of writing this book, I was one of the full-time elders at King's Church. At the beginning of 2009, I took on the leadership of Beacon Church, south central London, a church plant out of King's.) The second level of the journey is what I myself have observed in churches that I have visited over the years, particularly but not exclusively in London. The third level of the journey is what I have been told by church leaders and those who attend churches. What has been happening is basically this: churches all over the UK have started to grow in diversity, i.e. people from different ethnic backgrounds are beginning to attend churches made up of people not like themselves. The vast majority of these churches that I am aware of began predominately with white people attending, who have been joined by people from ethnic minority groups.

Experience

King's journey began a few years ago, when Lawrence and Mary Obodosike represented a new type of growth. The church already had a level of diversity, because for the last twenty years or so it was a mixture of white, black Caribbean and black British to the second generation (like me). However, Lawrence and Mary were the first black African family (they were from Nigeria) to attend the church. They represented not just a racial but also a more obvious cultural diversity. They didn't come to King's needing help, but in order to help and build friendships. Not long after they arrived, another group began attending: also black African and Caribbean from 'black majority churches'. One woman said to Steve Tibbert, our senior pastor, one day, 'I've never been in a church led by a white man before!' Something was beginning to change in the landscape of the church. Since then, diversity has increased, and it's not just more black Africans (who represent the largest single group of new people), but people from many different nations: China, Brazil, India, Colombia, white South Africans, Eastern Europeans and many others. A conservative estimate of King's congregation make-up would be at least forty different nations.

Observation

When I can, I love visiting other churches. It has become part of our family tradition that usually once or twice a year we visit another church. One of the things I have discovered as I have spoken to people during these visits is the growth in diversity, which they had never experienced before. I realize it is not just King's Church experiencing this new growth, but many other churches too.

Others' testimony

The testimony of many UK church leaders that I have spoken to or heard about, in part backed up by research done by Christian Research, is that churches are growing in diversity. I used to think this was true of a particular type of church, but I have begun to realize it is not: all groups are seeing growth in diversity. I am not necessarily saying that churches are getting larger, but in many cases the make-up of the community is changing.

This has led me to ask two questions:

Why are churches growing in this way?

There may be many reasons. God's plan, a preference for diversity and the impact of global migration are some that we will explore further in this book. However, here I just want to highlight some basic reasons, from what people have said to me.

- Location. Some people, particularly from minority groups, travel for thirty minutes or even up to an hour to get to the church they want to attend. Increasingly, however, they are beginning to go to their local churches, and the fact that it may be different from what they are used to is no longer an issue.
- Family reasons. More and more, children are the reason why people attend diverse churches. Children have asked why every other part of their lives is mixed, but when it comes to church everyone is the same!

- Leadership issues. Some people are leaving their
  historic churches as these churches have gone through
  leadership challenges and crises. In certain cases, people
  felt hurt or let down by their leadership.

How is the church responding to that growth?

- A positive welcome. Huge progress has been made
  in accepting people who are different. Churches have
  been overwhelmingly positive and very excited about
  growth. In some cases, they try to learn songs from
  different groups, erect flags that represent the different
  nations coming in, and host evenings to celebrate their
  diversity, with food and music.
- Beyond the initial welcome. Churches are not
  necessarily sure how fully to embrace diversity, both
  beyond the initial welcome and in aspects of church
  life such as leadership, worship, small groups and, most
  importantly, in personal relationships. So, many of these
  churches can look similar, and it would not be unusual
  to find a church with 25% or more of its congregation
  from different backgrounds, but its leadership, worship
  teams and the general feel or culture of the church
  remains that of one cultural group. Also, the diversity
  observed in the Sunday congregation often does not
  extend to the community life of the church, such as
  small groups and other ministries. Finally, diversity
  can be even less likely in the personal relationships of
  members and leaders.
- Theologically blind. I am not a theologian, but I have
  sought to raise numerous Bible references that touch
  directly on the issue of diversity. Often commentaries
  do not make reference to these issues, even though they

are clearly in the passage. In many cases, the meaning of a passage is not either/or, but both/and. Our theology of diversity is very general. Many of us have not yet seen or understood that diversity is pervasive throughout the Scriptures, and that there is a theology of diversity which begins in Genesis and finishes in Revelation. What we are seeing in our churches in terms of growth in diversity is something the New Testament church also experienced, and one of the main issues they grappled with. So it is to the Bible we must go for answers, to discover God's heart and plan. In so doing, we can fully embrace the diversity we see around us and take hold of the unique opportunity for the church.

So, if I were to attempt to sum up this book, I would say that diversity is at the heart of God's plan and purpose for the world. In order fully to embrace diversity, we need to be aware of the issues that have kept people apart: for example our histories, our prejudices and our lack of awareness and appreciation of our difference. Finally, we need to find ways and means now to overcome such barriers, build bridges and thereby create truly diverse churches that help us to reach across the divide. I will address all these issues.

I realize that, while many churches are growing in the area of diversity, not many are grappling with the associated issues, which is why I have written this book. I hope to help churches embrace what they are seeing and prepare for further growth.

Many of the examples and stories in this book come from King's Church, which ran a seven-week series on these issues in the early part of 2008. We used an excellent book called *Gracism: The Art of Inclusion*, by Dr David Anderson, a pastor in the USA who leads a large, diverse church in Baltimore, Maryland. Dr Anderson defines gracism in this way:

> Gracism unlike racism does not focus on race for negative purposes
> such as discrimination. Gracism focuses on race for the purpose
> of positive ministry and service. When the grace of God can be
> communicated through the beauty of race, then you have Gracism.

In the book, Dr Anderson takes a fresh look at 1 Corinthians 12:14–27, and comes up with the seven sayings of a gracist. During the series, a number of people in our church kept journals, some of whom were happy to be named, while others were anonymous. We were all encouraged to share our stories and testimonies of diversity. This happened both at our Sunday services and also in our small groups: never with the aim of a book in mind, but rather honest and at times raw reflections and comments, an attempt to get behind the face of diversity and discover some of the real issues. I have been given permission by those who kept journals and told their stories to reproduce them in this book, and I am very grateful. I hope you find these stories helpful. Some are very honest and direct. Some of my own reflections and comments are equally honest and at times direct. The aim is not to offend or single out a particular group, but to raise awareness and to learn.

Many people I have spoken to have rightly been quick to point out that there are other types of diversity besides racial and cultural diversity. Gender, age, class and disability are other aspects of diversity that we need to embrace, and I would encourage churches to do this. Crossing the Divide chiefly, although in no way exclusively, looks at issues surrounding race and culture. The main reasons for this are: first, that this is the new diversity that churches are experiencing and that we need to make room for. In fact, rightly or wrongly, many people refer only to diversity in church when referring to some form of racial or cultural mix. Secondly, I believe that to focus in on a particular aspect of diversity is a good thing, because many of the principles are transferable to other forms of diversity too, and there may be particular issues that need to be addressed in detail. Thirdly, I believe this approach is consistent with the way the Bible addresses these issues, something I will unpack later. Fourthly, there is no one right way to address such an issue, because, however you do it, some will feel that another way would have been better!

Therefore we must not lose sight of our overall aim and purpose, which is to help churches make room for and embrace the diversity they are seeing, because this is a testimony to the world of what Jesus ultimately achieved through his death on the cross: the reconciliation of people to God and to one another.

As John Piper says, 'Diversity magnifies the Glory of God now.'

1. WHY IS THE ISSUE OF DIVERSITY SO IMPORTANT TO THE CHURCH TODAY?

Inclusive living

My mother had a big influence on me. As a Christian, she was very inclusive in her relationships, and as a family we followed her example. Under her influence we never developed a 'them' and 'us' mentality in our relationships. It was quite normal for us to have diverse people groups in and around our house. Many were black West Indians, many were white, some were Asian and African, some working class and some middle class. All were welcomed, fed and loved. I don't think I ever heard her say anything that made me think there was a 'them' and an 'us' in the world. Unfortunately, I later acquired that way of thinking, but certainly not from her.

After I left home, mum carried on her inclusive living in south east London, fostering teenagers who had come from very difficult and sometimes abusive backgrounds. She never gave up on anyone. At her funeral, there were literally hundreds of people from every colour, creed and generation, celebrating the life and mourning the death of this sixty-one-year-old Jamaican woman. What my mum demonstrated in her life and at her funeral was this: it is possible to bring people from across the divides together as a true demonstration of Christian diversity in unity.

Integral to the design

We have recently had the joy of a new kitchen extension. From the outset, my wife Pauline had a very clear idea of what she wanted our new kitchen to include. We made plans, employed builders and started work. The new kitchen began to take shape. After some time, a new external wall began to emerge, with a space for a new back door. My wife looked at the wall space between the existing window and the newly formed doorway with suspicion. The plan showed that a cooker and a storage cupboard should inhabit this space. Our builder took out his tape measure. He confirmed that there was room for the cooker or the cupboard, but not both. Perhaps there was some room for manoeuvre? Pauline had given very careful thought to the layout of the kitchen. The position of these items was not just aesthetic, but integral to the smooth running of the kitchen. The back door was moved!

As it turned out, there were a number of things which my wife considered as integral to the design of our kitchen: a particular make of dishwasher, a specific type of fridge freezer, an exact style of tap. Things which I had naively thought would be just a matter of taste or preference were simply not open to negotiation! The whole family are now enjoying the benefits of our fantastic new kitchen, and I'm so pleased that Pauline stood her ground and didn't compromise over those things which she saw as being integral to its smooth running.

When it comes to the issue of diversity, we may ask a very similar question: how integral is this issue to the church today? Is it not just a matter of preference or taste? Is it more important for some churches and not so important for others? Does it depend on location, leadership style, leadership background and context, or is there more to it than that? If the church were stripped back to her bare necessities, would this be an element that we would be anxious to keep or happy to lose?

Whichever way you look at it, in the UK and elsewhere today, the issues of diversity, inclusion and integration are increasingly facing us all. Barely a day goes by when we do not read about these issues in our newspapers or watch news items relating to them on our TV screens. A recent article in the *Weekend Guardian* contained a series of short interviews with children born in every nation of the world, now resident in the UK. Of all the nations in the world, there were only seven that were either not represented or from which willing interviewees could not be found. The UK is really becoming a nation made up of all the nations of the world.

Growing diversity

Diversity is affecting our lives in a major way, and especially in our major cities and large towns. Having been born and brought up in London, I spent fourteen years working for a government department in the city centre. London is truly a world city. Among its millions of inhabitants are people from literally all over the world, all mixed up, and living in communities together. When my parents came to London in 1960, immigrants tended to cluster together in certain areas. That is no longer the case, as in almost every London borough diversity has increased in the last ten years. Today, 25% of all

Londoners were born abroad, and that doesn't include the thousands of people from ethnic minorities who themselves were born in London. Statistics tell us that 50% of all London's churchgoers are from ethnic minority communities. One could argue that, without the presence of ethnic minorities, church attendance in London would be in decline.

But the growth in diversity is not restricted to those traditional areas where ethnic minority communities are already well established. Diversity is breaking out into new regions. I personally know of churches in Bracknell, Woking, Reading, Newcastle and Teesside which, among many others, are growing in diversity.

Research shows us that, while overall church attendance has declined, in areas of the UK which are ethnically diverse it is actually growing. This is partly due to the fact that a greater proportion of ethnic minorities attends church than does the indigenous population. The church in the city and, indeed, across the nation has a unique opportunity to be a leading example when it comes to people building relationships across the divides.

Handling our differences

Around the world, communities have to deal with issues of difference and diversity all the time. This is in no way unique to the UK. Consider tribalism in some African nations, ethnic tensions in some Eastern Europe countries, race issues in the United States, and the caste system in India. Issues of diversity and difference are everywhere. How does the world deal with them?

In April 1990, within five months of the overthrow of President Ceauşescu, a group from King's Church, including myself, took food and supplies into Romania. As outside observers, it was interesting to see how ethnic and racial tensions flared up the moment the Communist political system broke down. Actually, Romania handled the challenges of changing from a Communist country after many years to a fledgling democracy better than some other countries. It was clear, though, that Communism had not dealt with the issues of diversity and difference. It had just suppressed them.

In some instances, the Western world has not fared much better. In parts of the USA you do not need to look very hard to pick up on the racial tensions and the unresolved issues of slavery and segregation that still exist. For example, on numerous occasions during the 2008 US presidential election campaign the issue of race was raised. I watched ordinary Americans saying they would not vote for Barack Obama because he was black. This is only one example of the fact that race remains an issue around the world today.

Today in the UK, tensions arising from issues to do with race and diversity can be far less obvious than in the past. People from minority groups are now protected by law from the worst forms of discrimination, and of course this is a good thing. If we scratch the surface, though, these tensions are often still there, albeit in subtler forms. For example, while people may live in the same communities, work together and send their children to school together, they very rarely socialize across communities. The reality is that most people choose to spend time with people like themselves. Although some people have relationships across the divides, the fact is that most of us don't. We can be friendly and polite, but when it comes to developing friendships, we tend to retreat to our comfort zones and stick with those similar to ourselves. Sometimes this can be our experience within church life too. People from very different backgrounds may attend the same church, but tend to socialize with people like themselves.

A Martian's response to the gospel

I don't believe there are aliens living on other planets, but humour me for a moment! Imagine, it's a Saturday morning and you're on your way to the supermarket when a Martian lands on the pavement right in front of you. 'Greetings!' he says. 'I'm on a mission to seek out life on other planets and to find out if there is a God who created the universe. Tell me, have you ever met God?' Wow, divine appointment or what! You've just completed some training in sharing your faith, so you're keen. Even better, this is a cross-species witnessing opportunity. Wait until you tell the members of your small group about this one!

So you tell the Martian about Jesus, that he is the Saviour of the whole world and also Lord of the universe. The Martian is interested! He says he believes. But before he's prepared to repeat the prayer at the back of the tract you've given him, he asks if there is anyone else he can check this story out with first. 'Sure,' you say, 'go and visit any church in the town and they'll tell you the same.' You are confident that on these basic doctrines, at least, they will all agree! You arrange to meet the Martian again in a week's time.

A week later you are shocked when the Martian tells you he no longer believes that all you told him is true. Trying to hide your disappointment (and secretly regretting having sent him to some of the other churches in the town which have clearly led him astray with weird doctrine), you ask the Martian what's happened to bring him to this conclusion. Was it the welcome he received in the churches he visited, or the lack of it? Was it the worship? Maybe it was the style or the content of the preaching? 'No,' the Martian replies. 'It was none of these things.' In fact, he had heard the same basic message that you had first told him in all of the churches he had visited.

'So can you explain to me what it is that's changed your mind?' you ask.

The Martian begins, 'Well, I went to one church and they were all white, to another church and they were all black, then to one church where they were all old, and to another where they were all young. It just seemed strange that if Jesus is the Lord of the universe, why didn't he bring all those people together? More importantly, which church am I supposed to attend?'

You are lost for words. You say that Jesus has done exactly that. He has made it possible for all these people to come together as one special, dearly loved people belonging to him. It's just that they often choose not to. They all worship and love and serve the same Lord Jesus. They just prefer to do so with their own kind. You try to explain some of the complexities of church history and culture, but you can see the Martian isn't convinced. And actually, neither are you.

If Jesus has completed such a defining work which reconciles us to God and to each other, why is his church sometimes so divided by race, age and culture? In *Gracism: The Art of Inclusion*, David Anderson says, 'One bride, not a harem, is what Jesus is coming back for.' Although we believe that Jesus is coming back for one bride, we sometimes do church as though he is coming back for many brides. We may say that we are getting ourselves ready, but we fail to realize that part of getting ready is being together.

The challenge to homogeneous churches

In the UK it is not uncommon for churches to be formed around a particular language, social status, people group or age group. People might say that, although there are different types of churches, the whole universal body of Christ is diverse. This view of churches being built around one particular group is being challenged today in three ways. First, by churches which display increasingly generational, social, racial and cultural diversity. Secondly, by a world grappling with the complexities of diversity, finding no answer, but sensing that the answer lies not in separation but in some form of integration. Thirdly, by a growing theological understanding that diversity in unity is part of the biblical basis for the church.

Having said all this, part of the uniqueness of Jesus is his ability to reach out to us wherever we are. But much more than that, he takes us out of our own cultures and subcultures and joins us to his culture, to his people, to his family – altogether different and unique. In King's Church we found that, as we grew in numbers, we also grew in diversity. We had many nationalities represented in the church and sought to become a truly multicultural church that reached across the divides. We were on a journey and we still had much to learn. Church had definitely become more complex, but it certainly felt more complete.

It is my personal conviction that the issue of diversity is integral to the Christian faith, to the church today and to a lost and divided world. I see it as an integral part of God's grand design and his purpose on the earth, not just for heaven and eternity. The issue of diversity touches God's very heart. One of the main purposes of this book is to show why diversity is so important and how we can demonstrate successful diversity in the church.

For the remainder of this chapter, let us look together at three areas in the Bible which underline God's heart for diversity.

Diversity in unity

> My prayer is not for them alone. I pray also for those who will
> believe in me through their message, that all of them may be one,
> Father, just as you are in me and I am in you. May they also be
> in us so that the world may believe that you have sent me. I have
> given them the glory that you gave me, that they may be one
> as we are one: I in them and you in me. May they be brought to
> complete unity to let the world know that you sent me and have
> loved them even as you have loved me.
> (John 17:20–23)

The phrase 'unity in diversity' or 'diversity in unity' is sometimes used to describe Christians coming together from different racial, ethnic, social or denominational back-grounds, expressing their unity as Christians. I am aware of churches and Christian groups in various towns and cities all over the UK that come together across the divides to work, pray, celebrate, or do mission together, in part to demonstrate our oneness in Christ. In recent years Festival Manchester, Soul in the City (in London) and Global Days of Prayer would be good examples of this. Such initiatives are on the increase and should be applauded and encouraged as positive expressions of unity.

In relation to the prayer that we are looking at, who was on Jesus' mind and heart when he prayed that most intimate prayer for all believers? I believe that, in his heart, he was thinking about more than denominations and Christian groups; that somehow he saw Christians from different gen-erations, races, cultures, classes and ethnicities together in unity, as a visible demonstration to the world of who he was and of what he had done. Unity was to be in relationships, not only in doctrinal statements or events. The apostle Paul exhorts the church at Ephesus to 'Make every effort to keep the unity of the Spirit through the bond of peace' (Ephesians 4:3). Unity in relationships was something they had to work on.

Let us consider whether we are following Jesus' model for unity or creating our own model. Our unity must go beyond what is humanly possible by our efforts and organization. It must instead demonstrate something of what only Christ could achieve through his reconciling death on the cross.

As international Christian statesman John Stott says,

> It is simply impossible, with any shred of Christian integrity, to go on proclaiming that Jesus by his cross has abolished the old divisions and created a single humanity of love, while at the same time we are contradicting our message by tolerating racial or social or other barriers within our church fellowship.

While we would find it hard to disagree with such a statement, could some of us admit that the reality of our lives actually suggests that it doesn't always change our behaviour?

Diversity in the Trinity

Jesus prayed for the unity of all believers to reflect the unity he has with the Father. He prayed that their unity would flow out of being in him, that it would be visible to the world, and by its very nature show the world who he was. Jesus anticipated this relational unity being something altogether different from other relationships and modelled on his own relationship with his Father. If we acknowledge the perfect unity in diversity demonstrated in the relationship of the Trinity – Father, Son and Holy Spirit – then we must seek in practice to copy it. Our relationships should be characterized by that which we see in the Godhead.

Jesus ascended into heaven, having achieved victory on the cross and in the tomb. He took with him, into the heart of God, one new humanity. Right at the heart of God is a diverse but united people. Let's look at a couple of characteristics of diversity in the Trinity that should be reflected in our relationships with one another across the divide.

Love

Weddings are great occasions. I remember quite clearly my own wedding day over seventeen years ago, and since then I have been privileged to conduct a number of weddings at the same church. The vows a couple make to each other on their wedding day are an important and powerful expression of their love, intentions and promises. However, the marriage relationship is not just a case of making statements on the wedding day. Somehow those sentiments, spoken at that most serious and yet joy-filled moment, must be backed up with visible and tangible expressions of love. I must demonstrate my love and commitment to my wife, whether she is sick or well, whether we are rich or poor, as long as we both live.

'This is how God showed his love among us: He sent his one and only Son into the world that we might live through him. ... Dear friends, since God so loved us, we also ought to love one another' (1 John 4:9, 11). What more tangible expression of love is there? In imitation, we must develop relationships across the divides which demonstrate visible and tangible expressions of love and commitment, not out of duty or expectation, but out of genuine love.

Submission

In Luke 3, at the baptism of Jesus, we see each member of the Trinity being fully who they are in relation to one another. We see the obedience of the Son to the Father, the approval of the Father to the Son and the empowering of the Son by the Spirit. For some of us, submitting to people who are different from us may be a humbling and challenging experience. We can be submissive by starting to recognize and acknowledge when our culture or values are being imposed on others. We can be submissive by not judging others by our own cultural standards or expectations.

Intimacy

Jesus' prayer in John 17 not only allows us to see those things which are important to him, but also gives us an insight into his relationship with his Father. It is a prayer of intimacy which comes out of an intimate relationship. Developing relationships across the divides should be characterized by intimacy, at a level where we can share and be open and honest about our concerns, worries, prejudices, hopes and dreams, without fear of being misunderstood or rejected. In Christ, such relationships are possible not just with those like us, but also with those who are different.

During the 'Gracism' teaching series at King's Church, some people began to find new levels of openness and vulnerability not known before, as people shared their stories and others listened. Here is an extract from a journal kept during the series.

Saturday 9 February

Chat with flatmate
We have both decided that we are going to ask our friends about their stories and experience of growing up as a black person in London. I have done this a little before but this series gives me the opportunity to go deeper. If I call these people my closest friends (which they are) then it's about time that I took a step

closer to finding out what it's like to walk in their shoes. I know
I won't be able to understand or experience all that they have
gone through (or go through) but I want to find out all that I
can and learn from it. I want to use my friendships as a 'safe
place' where I can test my thoughts, ask questions, communicate
objections and voice frustrations ... if they'll let me!

God's plan

Diversity was on God's heart from the very beginning, and
this can be seen throughout the Bible.

Diversity from the beginning

> So God created man
>   in his own image,
> in the image of God
>   he created him;
> male and female
>   he created them.
> (Genesis 1:27)

A greater understanding of this verse alone would help us to
establish our identity and our relationships. It would help some
to deal with deep-seated feelings of inferiority, and others to
deal with deep-seated feelings of superiority and pride.

We see the creation story as fundamental to everything
we believe. God created us male and female, which means all
human beings are valuable as people created in God's image.
Adam and Eve walked with God in the garden and enjoyed
his presence. Then temptation came.

> 'You will not surely die,' the serpent said to the woman. 'For God
> knows that when you eat of it your eyes will be opened, and you
> will be like God, knowing good and evil.'

> When the woman saw that the fruit of the tree was good
> for food and pleasing to the eye, and also desirable for gaining
> wisdom, she took some and ate it. She also gave some to her
> husband, who was with her, and he ate it.
> (Genesis 3:4–6)

One lie from the enemy, and pride rose in their heart. They believed that they could be like God and they sinned against God. As a result, Adam and Eve were subject to his judgment, which meant being sent away from his presence. Ever since that moment, sin has separated us from God: not only the sins of Adam but our own sins. That first sin of pride continues to be a major sin for many people.

Judgment at the Tower of Babel

> Now the whole world had one language and a common speech
> ... Then they said, 'Come, let us build ourselves a city, with
> a tower that reaches to the heavens, so that we may make a
> name for ourselves and not be scattered over the face of the
> whole earth.'
> But the LORD came down to see the city and the tower that the
> men were building. The LORD said, 'If as one people speaking
> the same language they have begun to do this, then nothing they
> plan to do will be impossible for them. Come, let us go down and
> confuse their language so they will not understand each other.'
> So the LORD scattered them from there over all the earth.
> (Genesis 11:1–8)

The account of the Tower of Babel is a parallel account to that of Adam and Eve, except with peoples and nations rather than individuals. Once again we see in this passage that pride is the main problem. It is the pride of the people that seeks recognition and creates a desire to build a tower to heaven and make a name for themselves. As a result of pride, God scatters the people across the earth and confuses their language as an act of judgment. Suddenly they find themselves divided and no longer able to relate to one another.

The key thing to note is that the Lord scattered them as an act of judgment resulting from their pride. It was God who created the earthly divisions and set the nations in place because pride was in the hearts of men. When I first recognized that it was the Lord who had scattered the peoples, I remember the sense of relief I had as I realized that God did it and he was responsible. Reassuringly, just as God scattered them, it is only God who can bring about reconciliation of the nations.

The promise to Abraham

In Genesis 12:1–3 we find that God's plan of redemption was not just for the individual, but for the nations, through the promise to Abraham: God promised Abraham that all nations would be blessed through him. What we see in Genesis 11, the scattering of the peoples because of judgment, is followed in Genesis 12 with the promise to Abraham of the blessing of the nations. God has always had the nations on his heart and this promise becomes like a central thread running right through the whole of the Bible. It is referred to and repeated in Genesis 26:24 and Psalm 72:17.

Diversity in the Gospels

God had a plan for the redemption of his people, to bring them back into a relationship with himself, and that plan was fulfilled in the sending of his Son Jesus into the world to pay the price for our sin and bring us back into a relationship with God.

John 3:16 summarizes God's plan perfectly: 'For God so

loved the world that he gave his one and only Son, that who-
ever believes in him shall not perish but have eternal life.'

In the New Testament, we see Jesus pointing towards a
reconciliation of the nations when he describes his house as a
house of prayer for all nations (Mark 11:17). Repentance and
forgiveness will be preached to all nations (Luke 24:47). Jesus
shows us again and again that he has the nations on his heart.
Later on, we will look specifically at other ways in which
Jesus clearly embraces diversity.

Diversity in the New Testament church

We then see in the account of Pentecost that 'Jews from
every nation under heaven' (Acts 2:5) were represented and
that they understood through the language of the Spirit.
Whereas God had once scattered the nations over the earth
and confused their languages, he now began the process of
restoring them to himself and to one another. Although at
Pentecost they were all Jews, they represented the nations
and clearly spoke different languages, representing God's
heart for diversity. They were no longer in separate and dis-
parate groups but coming together to form one body.

We must learn to see that people being baptized in the
Holy Spirit at Pentecost was only part of what was going on
there. Some commentators would argue that Pentecost was
the beginning of the fulfilment of the promise to Abraham
and also a reversal of the judgement at Babel.

In other parts of Acts, we find the church grappling not
just with issues of law and grace, but race, culture and class.
The dispute between the Greek and Hebrew widows is one
such example in Acts 6. Later we will look more closely at
this and other examples. Ephesians 3:10 reminds us that
God's purpose was to display his manifold wisdom through
the church, a gathered community of people from every

tribe, tongue and nation. Galatians 3:28 states our equality and unity in Christ as people: 'There is neither Jew nor Greek, slave nor free, male nor female, for you are all one in Christ Jesus.' Finally, in Revelation we catch a glimpse of the heavenly community, people from every nation and tribe together worshipping the Lamb on the throne.

To sum up ...

A well-known Christian leader from the United States once said to me that because of the pain and hostility associated with issues of racial division in the USA, he didn't believe that unity in diversity would ever be possible here on earth and that we would have to wait for heaven to experience it. I am pleased to say that he has changed his mind and is now fully committed to building churches that cross the divide. Clearly, we will never experience unity in diversity in all its fullness here on earth, but where sin abounds, grace abounds more, and much grace is needed to see more unity in diversity now.

Questions for discussion

In what ways has diversity affected your life?

How would you respond to the Martian?

Consider in what ways meditating on Genesis 1:27 can affect someone who may have feelings of inferiority or superiority. In what ways does this verse affect you? Write down any thoughts or feelings that come to you.

What do you think about the idea that diversity was on God's heart from the beginning of time? How does that influence your response to the growing diversity you see happening around you?

2. 'I THOUGHT WE WERE ALL THE SAME, SO WHAT'S THE ISSUE?'

Black guy, blue jeans!

What happened next was like a scene out of *The Sweeney*, *Starsky and Hutch*, *Miami Vice*, or perhaps just London. I was rushing to work in the middle of the afternoon, walking quickly towards the station. In a plastic carrier bag I had some car keys and a cheese knife. A car screeched to a halt, mounted the pavement a few yards in front of me, and out jumped two large men who made their way swiftly towards me. Fear gripped me, and I didn't have time to react before I stood face to face with the two men.

They turned out to be plain-clothed police officers. One of them flashed his card and said they were from the robbery squad, looking into a robbery which had just taken place in a post office not far from where I was standing. The suspect was described as a black guy wearing blue jeans. At first I didn't believe they were police officers, and I had never heard of the robbery squad. Also, there were loads of other black guys with blue jeans around! I remember asking a couple of times to check their warrant cards. At the same time, I was just a little concerned about what they might make of the contents of my plastic bag! I explained that the keys were for my mum's car which I had just dropped off at her place of work, and the knife was used to open boxes of wine and beer at the off-licence where I was employed, and it was in my bag by mistake! They checked my description and my story, and thankfully I was allowed to carry on my way. It was neither the first nor the last time I was to have this kind of experience.

No issue

As Christians we haven't always realized how much the Bible has to say about race and diversity. Our attitude to diversity and a theology of difference has historically been lightweight and based around two central scriptures: 'God created man in his own image' (Genesis 1:27) and 'There is neither Jew nor Greek, slave nor free, male nor female, for you are all one in Christ Jesus' (Galatians 3:28). Our interpretation of these two scriptures has been that, as we are all the same and we are all equal, there is no issue. I have had numerous conversations with people who believe that we are all the same: God is colour-blind and doesn't see our differences. He sees us as all the same, so what is the issue?

Of course there is an element of truth in this statement, because I believe we are all created in the image of God and we are all one in Christ. However, I do not believe that the conclusion of these truths is that diversity is not an issue and that God is colour-blind. It seems to me that in reality there is a little more to it than that. Our differences often have a very profound and real impact on our life experiences, choices and relationships.

A big issue

I grew up in a highly racialized environment and I have lived all my life within a few miles of the street where the teenager Stephen Lawrence was murdered in 1993. I remember the night when he died, and the days that followed it. I remember the bad taste his death left in the area, and the fear I felt, which was shared by others in the community, particularly the black community. As a teenager, I had been threatened on more than one occasion by skinheads. People I knew from school were involved in right-wing demonstrations for the National Front. I attended football matches where thousands of people made racist jibes at black players. I had been stopped and searched by police as a suspect in disorder offences and robberies, solely for being black and wearing blue jeans. In the world in which I lived, race was a big issue. In the church, however, race was not an issue. What I mean is that no one really talked or asked about it. Very few people would have understood the reality of my experience, and fewer still would have asked me about it.

Your story, my story?

On many occasions over the years people have said to me, 'I don't think of you as black, I think of you as Owen.' I believe that behind that comment is a veiled compliment, like, 'I just see you as you.' However, there is another side to it. First, by not thinking of me as black, which I am, the danger is that you may retain negative stereotypes about black people who look just like me, because you don't associate me with them. If you did think of me as black, it might just begin to adjust some of those negative stereotypes. Secondly, it may deny me the opportunity to relate the reality of some of my experiences of being black to you because you don't recognize that as part of who I am.

I once had a conversation with a pastor who said to me that he was trying to build a relationship with a member of his congregation from a different ethnic background to his own. He was describing how it was a slow process and at times quite hard work and he couldn't understand why this was. The man, the pastor said, was friendly enough and didn't appear to have any 'issues'. He went on to explain that what he meant by this was that his friend didn't appear to have a chip on his shoulder. I asked the pastor, 'Have you ever asked him to tell you his story?' He said he hadn't but that he would. The next time I saw the pastor, he informed me that when he asked the man about his story, he was quite overwhelmed by the number of experiences the man shared with him, which were a direct result of his being different. Many of these experiences the pastor would never have discovered, had he not asked him directly.

The reality of difference

Some of the people I most admire in our church are deaf. If you ever visit the home of a deaf person you will find various adjustments made to reflect the fact that they can't hear. Lights flash when you press the doorbell; subtitles are permanent fixtures when watching TV; fax machines are often fixed to telephones so that messages can be left. My wife keeps reminding me that, when a deaf person sends you a text message by mobile, you should reply straight away if possible, because they are not just leaving a message but having a conversation (a bit like you might have on the phone with a hearing person). I have found this to be wise advice.

We must face up to the reality of difference. The fact that I live next door to you or sit next to you on a Sunday at a church meeting does not mean that our experiences of life are the same, or that people respond to me in the same way as they respond to you. For many minority groups, be they ethnic groups, or those with English as an additional language, or individuals with a physical difference, there is the reality of difference every day.

Defining differences

The truth is that, for thousands of people, their difference defines them. It can be hard to recognize this when you are part of the majority group. We don't appreciate the adjustments that some people have to make every day, simply in order to make life work for them. Their outlook on life, their opportunities in the world, their friends, the place where they live and how people respond to them can be defined by their differences.

Let me give you a few real examples.

Name

Let me introduce you to Valerie. Valerie was born in the UK to Caribbean parents. She and her husband are part of my home church. This is her story in her own words:

Valerie Kwami

Valerie is an ordinary name. No-one struggled to pronounce my name. In fact I had English names, but when people saw me it was a different story. I spoke the same language, sang the same songs, ate the same food and we met in the same shopping centre. The problem was that I was a child in the wrong skin. I felt like a foreigner and it seemed as though my name had been changed for me. I met and married an African man and then my name changed. In my new world, with the African name, I was supposed to speak another language, sing different songs, eat different food and go to the market.

With a simple change of name, Valerie found that people's perception of her had also changed. In some cultures, when people come to the UK, they change names, shorten names or give themselves English-sounding names as a way of making it easier for people to identify with them. For example, Lou Ying is also known as Andrea. How many of us, if living abroad, would consider changing our name to fit in?

Skin colour

Wilben is from Sierra Leone. He is an active member of King's Church. He has held senior management and board positions in manufacturing, public transport operations and events management. In his current job he has overall responsibility for planning the transport for the 70,000 athletes, media and games organizers who will come to the London Olympic Games and Paralympic Games in 2012.

Yet Wilben has told me with a smile that, back in his days as a senior manager within London Underground, he lost count of the number of times that people would assume that he was a train driver or ticket collector! We may smile at this, but being on the receiving end of assumptions people make about us based on our skin colour can range from mildly frustrating to deeply hurtful and offensive. Skin colour can lead to people being ignored or treated with suspicion.

Accent

In *A Hitchhiker's Guide to the Galaxy*, a Babel fish is placed into the ear in order that different languages can be understood. How helpful that would be in a world growing in diversity, not just for languages but also for accents! Sometimes people speak and read English very well, but their accents remain strongly influenced by their background or country of birth. Occasionally we can respond negatively to someone's accent and equate a strong accent with poor command or a lack of understanding of the language, but that may not necessarily be true. Strong accents can require more concentration and patience to understand, but they are also part of the reality of growing diversity. We often joke with my brother-in-law about his accent. He was born and raised in Kent, but for the last ten years or so has lived in Greater Manchester. Every now and then, he speaks with a Mancunian accent!

Education

Whether you left school at sixteen or have a master's degree, your education goes before you. My wife and I recently finished watching a television series called *The Apprentice*, a reality show where contestants compete to win the chance of employment with one of Britain's most successful entrepreneurs, Sir Alan Sugar.

In this latest series, it emerged that the eventual winner had written inaccurately about his education on his initial CV. Despite having many evident business skills, his anxiety about his own perceived lack of educational experience had been so strong that it had led him to be less than honest when describing himself on paper. He seemed to worry that his apparent lack of formal qualifications would lead to his being discounted.

A large inner-city church recently conducted a survey of the educational attainments of its leaders. The results showed that the majority of members of the church's wider leadership team had been educated to degree level or above. Of course, the church had not required its potential leaders to submit a list of their qualifications before being considered for leadership! Nevertheless, these findings are interesting. Of course, there is much to be commended about pursuing a good education. I encourage my own children to do so. However, we should always be on our guard against education becoming an informal, almost unspoken prerequisite to leadership. This is especially important in days when churches are becoming increasingly interested in management and leadership models from the business world. Clearly, there are some helpful lessons to be learnt, but we must continue to make sure that we look first and foremost for biblical characteristics and gifting as the main qualification for leadership. God looks not on external appearances, but on the heart. The disciples Peter, James and John were fishermen, not educated high-flyers. Jesus himself was a carpenter. Yet Paul was indeed a man of learning. God anoints both types.

God sees our differences

How do we treat people who look, sound or act differently from us? If we are not careful, we can stereotype people because of their name, colour, accent or education. The alternative, though, should not be to over-simplify things by saying that we are all the same when we clearly are not.

God sees our differences. Not only is this true in people's life experience today, but the Bible also has many examples of people being defined by their differences. God is not blind to difference: he planned and created a world full of variety and diversity and he sees, acknowledges and embraces it. God accepts and uses people not just despite their differences, but because of them. The Bible is full of names and descriptions of people, and it often describes not just their name, but their ethnic background, gender and social status, even something of their character and personality. This is why we can identify so much with what the Bible says. It is primarily about God's dealings with people, people just like us. Let us look at a few real examples.

Rahab the prostitute

This woman, despite her social status, was considered right-eous (James 2:25). It is not insignificant that in the whole of Jericho the one person God saved was Rahab the prostitute, who risked her life to shelter the spies sent there by Joshua. Her background as a prostitute did not prevent her from being put forward as an example to us and included in the people of God. God is telling us something very profound about his ability to see, accept and use people according to his own purposes. He is not bound by our stereotypes of the people he might use.

Ruth the Moabitess

Ruth, a non-Israelite, was included in the royal line of Israel (Ruth 4:13, 17). As a Moabitess, Ruth was an outsider. There was historical tension and friction between Israel and Moab, which meant the two nations did not associate with each other. Yet she played a hugely significant role as the paternal great-grandmother of King David. When Matthew records the genealogy of Jesus, in order to show the Jews that Jesus was Jewish, he is also showing the Jews that God is not bound by culture or race, because Ruth the Moabitess, an outsider, is also listed there.

The rich young ruler

Jesus disappointed a young man who came to him to ask about eternal life (Matthew 19:16–22). The man is identified in the narrative by his wealth, age, status and gender, all of which would have been seen as positive and worthy creden-tials for one seeking eternal life, in the mind of the Jews. But Jesus told him that none of those things are important when it comes to eternal life.

The Ethiopian eunuch

The story of this man's faith shows us that the gospel is for everyone (Acts 8:26–40). An outsider by virtue of his race and his sexuality, he was nevertheless searching for truth. As a eunuch (a castrated male), he would not have been viewed as being a part of the people of God. In Deuteronomy 23:1 eunuchs are excluded from joining the people of God. However, this remarkable encounter with Philip led to the Ethiopian eunuch hearing and responding to the gospel. In ancient writings, Ethiopia was considered the ends of the earth. By reaching the Ethiopian eunuch, God shows early in Acts that his love extends to the ends of the earth.

God sees our differences, and that is why it is important that we acknowledge and embrace them in other people and in ourselves.

God accepts our differences

It is in this context of seeing our differences that verses like Galatians 3:28 make the most sense. There are in fact Jews, Greeks, slaves and free people, males and females. The point is that all these people can find oneness in Christ, not that they lose their identities. God embraces their differences and makes them one.

As 2 Corinthians 5:17 says, 'If anyone is in Christ, he is a new creation; the old has gone, the new has come!' We all become new creations, and if nothing else, this means that our primary identity is in Christ. So if I am deaf, I become a Christian who is deaf rather than a deaf Christian. Being a Christian becomes the primary thing, but I don't lose my identity. When I first had this revelation that my identity was first and foremost in Christ, it was incredibly releasing. I had struggled with identity for years, not appearing to be one thing or the other. I was born into a black West Indian family, but lived primarily in a white British world and never felt entirely accepted in either place. As a teenager, I grappled with this for years, as do many people from ethnic minority backgrounds who are born in the UK. I remember thinking to myself that I was not black enough yet clearly not white. When I accepted that I was a new creation because of what Christ had done for me, I thought of my new identity as being a Christian. From then on, I knew what I was, a Christian, and I found my primary identity in Christ. That brought about a great sense of release, as I felt free from any cultural expectations to be somebody or something in order to fit in. What mattered was that I was first and foremost in Christ. Clearly, this does not mean that I lose my cultural heritage, or that my cultural heritage is unimportant. On the contrary, it is very important, but understanding it as secondary to my identity in Christ is equally important.

We must accept our differences

Sometimes, in our desire to accept people and make them feel welcome and at home, we have denied or ignored their differences, which in turn can remove something of the unique contribution they can bring. On the other hand, in our desire to accept people as they are, we can over-emphasize their differences when they just want to fit in! God is a God of diversity: we see he is God in three persons, Father, Son and Holy Spirit, in perfect unity and relation-ship with one another. We must discover what it means to grapple with and embrace the reality of difference, not deny it, ignore it or over-emphasize it.

Accepting our differences raises a number of other issues, which I will attempt to break down in the remainder of this chapter:

Legislation

The importance of some of our current legislation lies in the fact that it acknowledges difference and seeks to protect the weak, the vulnerable and minority groups. We can sometimes look negatively on legislation which promotes and protects diversity. We can be sceptical of political correctness, equal opportunities and positive discrimination, seeing them as unfair and giving special treatment to one group over another. When asked about the value of legislation, Martin Luther King said, 'It may be true that the law cannot make a man love me, but it can restrain him from lynching me.'

Legislation as it relates to diversity is about protection, acknowledgement and promotion. It makes us aware that people are different. It does not necessarily help us to accept or embrace those differences (in fact, sometimes it actually does the opposite). People will never love one another across the various human dividing walls of hostilities just because the law says they should, but the law does highlight the fact that people can be treated differently. The law at least gives value to difference. The church, however, is called to far more than that. For us, it is not legislation that motivates, but the cross which bridges the divide and makes peace. What the law is powerless to do, Christ did by making peace between people on the cross.

Acknowledging difference

People may not like to acknowledge that they are different and often don't like to talk about their experiences of difference. This may be because they want to fit in and to do so is to minimize differences. Often people's experience of being different can be negative, so it can be too painful to recount their stories and they bury them deep inside and try to move on. Burying or ignoring our problems is not necessarily the best solution. No wise marriage counsellor would recommend that you bury your problems deep inside and try to ignore them. For a marriage to work well and for a couple to grow closer together, issues, however painful, must come out and be shared. The same is true in relationships across the divide: differences need to be worked on, trust built up and issues talked about.

Celebrating difference

'God saw all that he had made, and it was very good' (Genesis 1:31). God takes pleasure in his creation. Full of diversity, difference and variety, it was worth celebrating and taking a day off for! One of the strongest reasons for acknowledging our differences is to celebrate them with one another. Celebrating difference is another way of appreciating what God has done in making creation diverse, and also is a great way of uniting us.

To sum up ...

We are not all the same. We are not all treated the same by everyone we meet. If we are honest with ourselves, we also treat and respond to people differently.

One of the fundamental issues in building a diverse church is difference. The issue is not primarily racial barriers, but differences across the board and how we handle them. It is my belief that, if we can find ways of understanding, embracing and celebrating our differences at a more fundamental level, people from more diverse backgrounds will join our churches. Then we will all be blessed and God will be more glorified.

Questions for discussion

Name, colour, accent and education are all real differences. Which one of these do you think affects you most?

In what ways can we learn to appreciate differences in people around us?

How can we celebrate our differences?

3. WHAT ABOUT OTHER FORMS OF DIVERSITY? WHY FOCUS ON RACIAL DIVERSITY?

Progress

There has been much progress in the UK in different areas of diversity. Let me give you a few examples.

Sport

The summer of 2008 offered a feast of sport for those who love the Olympics as I do. I truly enjoyed watching the Beijing Olympics and celebrating the success of the British athletes. Roll on, London 2012! Following the Olympic Games in Beijing came the Paralympics, in which the world's best disabled athletes competed. In many ways these games were every bit as exciting and gripping to watch. In Dame Tanni Grey-Thompson, Great Britain has one of the world's best Paralympians ever. Much of the Paralympics was shown on the BBC and often featured in the news. Not too many years ago, such an event might have been unheard of, but progress is being made in the profile and awareness of disabled sport.

A little bit closer to home in a sense, for me, were the 2005 Deaflympics, in Melbourne, Australia. A deaf woman whom I have got to know over the years, Esther Maycock, was playing in the Great Britain women's football team which won the bronze medal. Esther is a Christian who not only reaches across the divide into the hearing world, but also seeks to reach out with the love of Christ to deaf people who are not Christians. The Deaflympics were unique, in that they were administered and organized by deaf people for deaf athletes to compete in. Around seventy nations and over 6,000 athletes took part.

In the mid-1980s, I was at college in Woolwich studying for my 'O' levels and in my class was Hope Powell. Hope is the first female manager of the England women's football team. To my knowledge, she is also the first British-born black manager of any national team!

Education

I could also give examples of progress in awareness of diversity in education, where schools employ special needs teachers, learning mentors and teaching assistants, as a result of recognizing that children don't all learn at the same rate and in the same way. Particularly in the cities, schools have an awareness of new children coming in, not only from other schools around the nation but from other nations around the world.

A few years ago, I would not have been able to cite so many different examples, mainly because there weren't many, but also they because they would not have been seen as newsworthy items in and of themselves. Great Britain as a nation has become very accommodating of people who are different.

Progress in the church

I recently spoke at a church weekend away on the subject of diversity, a first for me. The weekend had been entitled 'Making Room', which I thought was appropriate. While the church was not particularly large, over 50% of those attending the actual weekend event had been born in other nations around the world. The new eldership team spanned three continents with their different racial and cultural backgrounds. This church's experience is not unique, in the sense that many churches are making room for diversity. The leader was a gracious and humble man, well aware of his lack of awareness in certain areas and yet demonstrating a real desire to embrace diversity where possible. I am interested in seeing how his and many other churches around the nation make room for diversity.

Evangelical Alliance

I remember the day I first heard that Joel Edwards had become General Director of the Evangelical Alliance. I was so thrilled and excited that I joined the Evangelical Alliance on the spot. For me, it was a huge statement of progress and purpose that this predominately white British Christian institution had employed a black pastor from the Caribbean to lead them. Since then, I have met Joel on a number of occasions and he has been a great example and encouragement to me personally, and someone who has built bridges across racial and ethnic divides. Joel now works for Micah Challenge, an organization seeking to cut global poverty in half by 2015.

ESOL Alpha

For a number of years our church has from time to time run an Alpha course for English Speakers of Other Languages. In recent years, Alpha UK have launched an ESOL course for churches to use with people learning English, a great tool which potentially helps many churches to begin to embrace the diversity they are experiencing.

Newfrontiers

Newfrontiers, a family of churches based in the UK, began as a movement in the late 1970s. Now it has churches in every continent of the world. In recent years, local church projects and ministries that reach the most marginalized and vulnerable in society have begun to spring up. In the UK, churches work with asylum seekers, refugees, homeless people and single parents. They give debt advice and run pregnancy advice centres. A friend of mine now runs the annual Newfrontiers Social Action Conference, which seeks to equip and envision churches and individuals to reach out to marginalized and vulnerable people.

These are all encouraging signs that the church is growing in its awareness of diversity and that, in different ways, we are seeking to make room for diversity. Another area in which the church has to make room for diversity is in the area of singleness.

Growing singleness

Have you ever noticed how many churches use the word 'family' in their name? It can be 'Catford Family Church', or something like that. I wonder what this communicates to people who don't consider themselves to be part of a family. Do they think, 'Great, I can be part of a family!' Or do they think, 'That church isn't for me as I don't have a family.' The question might be, 'Do I need to be in a family to get in?' or 'Do I become part of the family when I join?' What is the natural bias of the church you are a part of? The question regarding the family church is something many people may face, though I imagine it may be a question single people face more than others.

It is difficult to determine what 'normal' church is, but many churches are based around, or run by and set up for, married couples with children. Often church programmes run according to school terms. This is not because it is the biblical approach, but because it takes into account the fact that at the church's core there are families who go away during the school summer holidays or at half terms. This is not necessarily the case among black and other ethnic minority churches or families, whose holidays may not be determined so much by school terms as by trips abroad to visit family at Christmas or on other such special occasions.

The apostle Paul addresses single people in 1 Corinthians 7:7–8: 'I wish that all men were as I am. But each man has his own gift from God; one has this gift, another has that. Now to the unmarried and the widows I say: It is good for them to stay unmarried, as I am.' Paul's personal preference was for single people to remain single, but he does also acknowledge marriage as a gift from God.

In Britain today the number of single people is on the increase. A few years ago, a British government survey estimated that by 2020, one in three people would not only be single but live alone. Mark Driscoll, leader of Mars Hill Church in Seattle, USA, said that half the congregation of the church he leads are single. The church I was a part of, until recently, would have a similar percentage. I think this probably applies particularly to churches in cities and large urban areas, where many single people move for work and also in order to find community.

Not only is the number of single people on the increase, but diversity among singles is also increasing. Single people in churches are no longer just those who have never been married, but also those who are divorced or separated, those not yet divorced, widows, widowers and those who are single parents. Another group of single people I have observed are what I would call economic or migrant singles. There is a growing number of people arriving in the major cities of the world such as London, for work or further education, as asylum seekers or refugees, without their wives/ husbands or families. This is not merely for a few weeks, but sometimes for years at a time. Certainly, at King's Church we had single people in this category. One man attended our church for two years before his wife was able to join him from Zimbabwe. Their children still remain in Zimbabwe with other extended family members.

Here are two implications for the church for the growing number of singles:

Ministry development

We need to ensure that single people feel part of the church and are able to access areas for ministry and leadership development. Two of the most gifted leaders I know are single: one a male in his forties, the other a female in her twenties.

Dating

We need to encourage singles to meet one another. As most churches are led by men with families, we can sometimes lose the priority of helping singles to meet. Singles find it difficult to meet other singles, and therefore meeting potential marriage partners is an increasing challenge. Also, churches often have many more single women than men, which only adds to this challenge. Some single women I know have taken radical steps such as joining Christian dating agencies or going Christian 'speed dating'. At least three Christian married couples I know met in this way!

Women

The role of women in the church and discrimination against women are other major issues. These are vast subjects, which I do not intend to tackle directly in this book. However, I do feel that many of the principles relating to other types of diversity relate here also.

Whatever your theological conviction on the role of singles and women in the church, two questions need to be asked. Do both groups feel valued in church because of the contribution they make? Are both groups fulfilling their God-given potential in the church?

The 'new diversity'

The 'new diversity' which society and the church needs to make room for is in the area of ethnic and racial diversity. It is in this area that many churches are experiencing growth. People are not only coming as a result of a felt need which makes them seek help from ministries offered by churches, but are themselves coming to help and to serve. They have a desire to join in and be part of church and to develop relationships. Although, on the face of it, the need for change is not always apparent, fully to embrace this diversity does require change in the way the church does things. It may also involve the church facing up to its history, reviewing processes and dealing with prejudices. So the focus is on racial and ethnic diversity. My hunch for the last few years has been that churches in the UK have been growing in this area, something confirmed by the national one-day conference we ran at King's Church on building multicultural churches, an event attended by over seventy churches and hundreds of people from all over the UK. Also, judging from my experience and conversations with numerous church leaders, growth in this area is widespread.

So why focus on race?
History
It is certain that some forms of slavery still continue today, although enslaving whole people groups came to an end well over a hundred years ago. However, the impact and effect of the latter is still felt by some people today as if it happened to them yesterday. This may well be something which people need to 'get over', but actually they may require help to do this. In a later chapter, I will seek to address how we go about this.

Personal experience
Some people in our churches will have been victims, or even perpetrators, of racism. They may have been in an environment where racist attitudes and even conduct were part of their day-to-day experience.

Emotional legacy
The experiences some people in churches have gone through may have left them feeling pain, guilt, anger, resentment or bitterness. These may be affecting how they live or act and whom they develop relationships with.

Politics
Race has become a political issue. Legislation and new guidelines are regularly being updated and introduced. While some of us assent on the outside, internally we react differently to the politics of race.

A racialized worldview

It may appear to some that the whole way society is set up seems to favour one race over another or one group over another. In part, it appears this way because certain jobs, roles or tasks appear to be administered or filled only by certain types of people.

Complexity

The issues surrounding race can be more complex than we realize. For some of us, it is the complexity itself that puts us off, as we would prefer simple, straightforward answers. We can get frustrated when they don't seem possible, and we may think people are making a mountain out of a molehill.

In the UK today, it is unacceptable to be racist. People can lose their jobs and ruin their reputations if they make comments, even out of complete ignorance, that are perceived to be racist. Other people unfortunately use this highly sensitized situation to play the 'race card'. They accuse others of being racist when they are not, in order to suit their own purposes and ends. As a result, people can be very fearful about what they say or don't say and to whom. No-one wants to be labelled, or admit to being, a racist. I wouldn't want you to think of me as sexist or ageist, but I would probably react most strongly if there was any hint that you thought I might be a racist.

An honest reflection

This is an extract from a journal written by a lady in our congregation as we worked through the 'Gracism' series at King's Church:

> Eighteen months ago I would not have considered I had a
> need for this teaching series. I have black friends that I love.

I deliberately live in London so that my children grow up surrounded by different cultures. When I am on holiday in whiter areas of Britain I miss the black faces (whilst loving the green fields and fresher air!). I felt in 1994 a burden to pray for a truly diverse racial mix of people in King's and I see today the answer to that prayer.

In 1995 I visited a number of Black African churches just to experience the way they worship and the incredible way they pray – often there were less than six white faces in a sea of black and I loved every minute of it (except once when no-one sat near us and I wondered why . . .).

I have been on dates with absolutely charming and gorgeous black men. So I can't be racist in the least, can I?

I do occasionally find black facial expressions disconcerting, usually a lack of expression which perhaps means discomfort or pain being hidden, I don't know. I find it a little intimidating and stay clear, I suppose because I can't read their faces so well. Even black friends I have known a long time sometimes have a sort of shut-down face and I haven't up until now ever talked about race with any of them.

I truly don't understand why race is such an issue for (it seems) black people. I am not sure it is an issue for white people. In the States, especially in the South, it is I know . . . but here in the UK? Well OK, here it must be since there are racially related attacks on the news, but in the church? Our church?

That's naïve, isn't it? If it exists in the world, it must also exist in the church. I just don't like to think that. Perhaps racism in the church is not so obvious, not violent, but perhaps hidden beneath smiles and attitudes and ignorance.

I do feel unable to say or ask about the race/colour issues I have, for fear of being perceived a racist, or perhaps for fear of discovering I am a racist . . . It has become painfully clear to me during this series that I am a racist.

Ouch. I want to rewrite that sentence so it is less harsh, but it is clear that, in my thoughts even if nowhere else, I treat some people differently, expect less of them or worse of them, or just expect not to understand them and be happy to let them do their thing while I do mine.

I have a great deal of respect for such an honest reflection on the complex issues surrounding race in the journal above.

An issue denied

We've touched on some of the reasons why talking about race can be emotive and sometimes feels like you're entering a minefield without the aid of body armour! Perhaps it is for this reason that people sometimes don't want to admit that race is an issue, when it is. We may explain away the fact that our friends all come from the same ethnic group as us by saying that they happen to be the people who live locally and with whom we seem to have most in common. We may say that the fact that our church leadership team doesn't seem very reflective of the racial mix of our congregation is because we look first for anointing (albeit looking for that anointing from the same direction each time!). Perhaps, like the journal writer above, we've not even been aware that some of our prejudices existed until we started to examine ourselves, as she did during our 'Gracism' series.

The organization I worked for before I became a full-time pastor had a race issue. For years, it was clear in the organization that some teams and groups had divided over race. Some people had been discriminated against and certain roles and tasks appeared to be filled only by certain people. At the other end of the spectrum, some people would 'play the race card' to further their own ends. The organization tried for years to grapple with these issues in many and varied ways. Finally, after I had left, the organization acknowledged that it had a race problem. And a bit like the alcoholic who first admits he has a problem with drink, admitting the problem was the first sign of real progress in this organization, and in many ways it became the first point of real change.

Racism is sin

Of course, racism isn't the world's biggest problem. Sin is. It is sin that separates us from God and causes us to be subject to his anger. We live in a world where the consequences of sin are all around us. Sin is the reason why AIDS has spread, people die in poverty, children are abused, marriages end in divorce, companies value profits over people, and people hate one another enough to kill one another.

And it is sin which causes people to think and react negatively towards other people, feel superior and choose not to develop relationships across the divides. Racism is sin, just as uncontrolled anger is sin. As we've seen, our society views racism as unacceptable. So, as a result, it is rarely an issue that surfaces in terms of what we say, because we've all learnt to be more guarded than that, but it can often surface in more subtle ways, such as our thoughts, attitudes and the choices we make about people every day.

Let me make this close and personal. I have struggled myself with racist thoughts and attitudes. It is not that I am negative towards everyone in a particular race or group, but I know that sometimes I have negative attitudes towards a group and I need to admit it to God and ask for his forgiveness. I have found this insight from the great Russian novelist Alexander Solzhenitsyn helpful: 'The line separating good and evil passes not through states, nor between classes, nor between political parties, but right through every human heart.'

Many of us may struggle at times with negative feelings towards other people who are not like us. Admitting that this is true is a major part of dealing with it. I want us to look at an example from the Bible.

How did Jesus deal with racism?

In Matthew 10:2-4 we read the names of Jesus' disciples: 'first, Simon (who is called Peter) and his brother Andrew; James son of Zebedee, and his brother John; Philip and Bartholomew; Thomas and Matthew the tax collector; James son of Alphaeus, and Thaddaeus; Simon the Zealot and Judas Iscariot, who betrayed him.'

Jesus surrounded himself with a diverse group of disciples. The Jews were God's chosen people, yet their land was occupied by the Romans. Feelings and attitudes both of superiority, because they were God's chosen people, and inferiority, for being under Roman occupation, would have existed in many of their minds. Jesus' disciples would have had the same attitudes as anyone else. There would have been extreme views among the twelve disciples Jesus chose.

While they were all Jews, Simon the Zealot was part of a Jewish revolutionary group which was known for using violence to oppose Roman rule in Palestine. Today we would see him as an extremist, quite possibly a racist or a terrorist. His views and attitudes would not be acceptable in mainstream society. At the other end of the scale was Matthew the tax collector. Matthew not only didn't oppose Roman occupation but was working for an occupying force that enforced the oppression of his own people and from which he benefited. No doubt Simon saw Matthew as a 'sell-out', and Matthew saw Simon as a bigot. Almost certainly, these two individuals would normally never have chosen to spend time together.

Jesus did something quite unique. He didn't just call them to be with him (Mark 3:13) but he called them to be together. When we take a closer look at these two disciples, we can begin to see how Jesus took two men of such extremes and turned them into a family, united in love for each other. This love involved serving and preferring each other and was demonstrated by the washing of each other's feet (John 13:14–15). Only Jesus could have done that. What Jesus did on earth among his disciples was to be an example for us to follow. He showed us that in him, and only in him, can relationships across the divides truly exist. Jesus is still teaching his disciples to love one another today. Are you actively seeking to build relationships with people who are very different from you?

The extremes of racial diversity

In his book *Multicultural Ministry*, David Anderson speaks about the bookends: the two ends of the spectrum, the extremes of racial diversity. Racial tensions between black and white have remained the hardest to resolve. If the church can really deal with the race issue with regard to black and white, this will help us to deal with all other forms of difference. We will learn to value and appreciate people for who they are and for what they may bring.

The Jew and Gentile issue

For us, the two 'bookends' of racial diversity are black and white, with unresolved issues that cause us to focus on this particular relationship. When we look at the New Testament, we find that the relationship which the apostle Paul focused on was that between Jew and Gentile. We see evidence of this throughout Paul's ministry. In the account of the Council of Jerusalem debate, in Acts 15, we read that some believers felt that the Gentiles needed to be circumcised and obey the Law of Moses in order to be saved. Paul argues that their inclusion among the people of God was not because of adherence to the law, but through grace and faith in Jesus. In Romans 15, Paul refers to himself as the apostle to the Gentiles and, as he addresses them, he reminds them that they have been grafted into the vine. When writing to the church in Galatia (Galatians 2), Paul tells how he rebuked Peter for withdrawing from table fellowship with the Gentiles for fear of the Jews. His words are strong: he actually tells Peter he is not acting in line with the gospel. Furthermore, he argues strongly that the Gentiles are saved by faith in Jesus alone, not by works of the law. In Ephesians 2, Paul puts the Jew/Gentile question at the very core of the gospel by claiming that it is through the blood of Christ that reconciliation is achieved and that God has created one new humanity.

Paul does address other forms of diversity also. He addresses issues relating to slaves and free, male and female (in Galatians 3:28) and barbarian and Scythian (in Colossians 3:11). In both passages, Paul effectively argues that there is no distinction between these groups in terms of their status before God, and that unity is found in Christ.

To sum up ...

Throughout the New Testament we find the issue of diversity addressed. Paul knew that to give ground on this, and to allow one group to assume dominance over another, would have had an impact on everything else. The fundamentals of the gospel were at stake. As the make-up of our churches changes, and as we seek to reach people from the different people groups in our increasingly diverse society, the time is right for us to take a step backwards and, in the light of our inclusive gospel, look again at what and how we're building.

Jesus died that we might be reconciled to God and to one another. Jesus said, 'My house will be a house of prayer for all nations' (Mark 11:17). In our generation and in our churches, more than at any other time to date, we have the potential to see these words being fulfilled.

Let's build wisely!

Questions for discussion

Can you think of other ways in which the church has made progress in the area of diversity?

Can you think of other areas in which the church needs to make progress in the area of diversity?

In what ways can churches ensure that the growing numbers of single people are included?

How does understanding racism as sin affect your view of it?

Think about the racial make-up of your three or four closest friends. What are the similarities and the differences, and why do you think that is?

4. WHAT ABOUT HISTORY AND ISSUES OF LEGACY?

History shapes you

In October 2004 I visited Cape Town, South Africa, with a couple of other leaders from my church. There, we managed to visit Robben Island, the place where Nelson Mandela and many other political prisoners were incarcerated during the apartheid years. The prison there had become something of a museum since the end of apartheid.

One of the most interesting aspects of our trip to Robben Island was meeting the tour guides. The men who showed people around the cell blocks and exercise areas of the prison had themselves been prisoners on Robben Island, and some had been political prisoners. They showed tourists not only where Nelson Mandela and Walter Sisulu had lived, slept, washed and exercised, but also where they themselves had lived. They were part of the history they were now recounting.

At the end of the tour, we approached our guide to ask him a question. Why, having been a prisoner on the island, did he choose to come back there to live and work? He talked about being released from prison and going back home. There were no jobs, no prospects, no counselling or help to rehabilitate him back into society. He struggled to deal with his own emotions and feelings about the past. He came back as a guide partly because he needed a job, but also because he found that retelling his story and answering questions from the many (mainly white) visitors to the island was in some way therapeutic. It helped him deal with his own responses to his past.

I couldn't help but see the irony of a man choosing to live on the same prison island that had once held him against his will. Not only that, but living on that island, and telling people the story of when he was a prisoner there, helped him deal with his past. It reminded me of how history so often isn't the past, but affects our present and shapes us. We can see this very clearly in the life of the tour guide on Robben Island, but also in our own lives.

Another example of how history not only shapes individuals but nations for centuries is found in the film *Kingdom of Heaven*, which is set at a time just before the Christian crusades. Orlando Bloom plays a soldier who manages to save the people of Jerusalem, although losing the city in the process. Though it is a film produced for entertainment purposes, and there was probably no such person as the character played by Orlando Bloom, it was also a film about a real period in history. At the end of the film, just before the credits, these words appear on the screen:

> The King, Richard the Lionheart, went on to the Holy Land and crusaded for three years. His struggle to regain Jerusalem ended in an uneasy truce with Saladin. Nearly a thousand years later, peace in the Kingdom of Heaven remains elusive.

I remember thinking, 'Wow! This is a historical event which occurred nearly a thousand years ago, but it continues to shape the present.' History really does shape us.

An invisible history

Our histories are very important to us. Where we come from matters in so many ways and can even determine our future. More and more, people are trying to trace their ancestry and family backgrounds. Where did I come from? Who were my ancestors and what did they do? History can stir in us deep emotions of pride, joy and confidence. It can also make us feel guilty, bitter and ashamed. Rarely does history fail to have an impact on us. Sometimes it is not just our recent and personal history that shapes us, but our nation's history, or the history of our race. The history of our ancestors becomes part of us. Furthermore, how that history is retold can affect us.

Sometimes our personal history in national historical events is almost invisible, but it can still make an impact on the way we live today. As a British-born son of Jamaican immigrants, I can only trace my history back a generation or so. I know my great-uncle Charlie (my grandmother's younger brother) came to Britain to serve during the Second World War. I also have a picture of my great-grandmother, who raised my mother. My dad has a mixed heritage which also includes South American Indians. It is estimated that 98% of Jamaicans are descended from slaves taken from West Africa. This is part of my history and consistent with what my parents have told me. My personal history is almost invisible, in that I can't trace my own history back to a particular person, tribe or even country. But I know that my ancestors would have been in the mix of slaves brought from West Africa during the transatlantic slave trade.

A shared history

In March 2007, the UK commemorated the two hundredth anniversary of the abolition of the slave trade. Nationally, this involved retelling the story of the transatlantic slave trade and the part the UK played both in it and in bringing it to an end. The commemoration also involved a call for putting an end to slavery today. At King's Church, among a congregation of forty-plus different nationalities, there were many of us who were impacted directly by that history. We put on our own presentation, called 'Freedom'. We told the history of the slave trade and also looked at the legacy of slavery, and we celebrated the fact that God had called us all to be together. There was not one person present who could trace their personal history either to that of a particular slave or slave owner, or to someone who had benefited directly from slavery. Our personal histories in that sense were invisible. We were not describing events that we had either witnessed or experienced for ourselves, as the transatlantic slave trade had ended 200 years ago. Yet retelling the story raised all sorts of very real and deep emotions for many people. This was particularly the case for white people from the UK and black people from the West Indies and some West African countries; we knew we shared this history together.

Different responses to history

Although we shared this history, our response to it was very different. After the 'Freedom' event, the strongest emotion many white people seemed to feel was guilt. A deeper emotion I observed was anger, which seemed to surface as a result of the feeling that they were being made to feel guilty about the past. Their strongest desire was for black people to move on from the past, forgive, look to the future and acknowledge how much progress had been made since the abolition of the slave trade.

A white woman at King's Church wrote in her journal:

> We had the celebration last Easter (March 2007) of the abolition of the slave trade. That was both brilliant and annoying from my perspective. The presentation was brilliant and it was good to identify with something so relevant to our community in terms of current affairs ... But ... it's historic, isn't it? When is everyone gonna get over it? That was what I really wanted to ask someone, only it's not very 'PC'. I did learn that the City of London was built from the wealth made by slaves, and that to some extent we owe our place in the world economy to slaves. Not good. Not proud of that. Still history though. Isn't it? At Easter, why didn't we focus more on slavery around the world today? It still exists. Do something. Instead of digging around in ancient sin and old pain. Or am I just entirely and completely missing the point? Probably.

For many black people, their strongest emotion was pain. Deeper emotions were bitterness and resentment, not so much because of what had happened to their ancestors, but because for them the legacy of slavery remains an unresolved issue. Their strongest desire was for white people to acknowledge and understand the past and recognize their value to society. At one point during the evening, a young black African got up and began to dance spontaneously in time with the music. The auditorium was dark, and you could just see the silhouette of him dancing against the stage lights. It was one of the most powerful moments in the presentation. When I spoke to him afterwards, he said he had just been so overcome with emotion that he had to dance, and that as he danced, he wept.

An unresolved issue and legacy

The abolition of the slave trade, achieved on 25 March 1807, was a momentous occasion in the history of the UK and the world. It ultimately led to the end of slavery as a legal enterprise all over the world. However, abolition had its limitations, and it never led to the immediate release of African slaves. That was to happen twenty-six years later, in 1833, when slavery itself was outlawed. Slaves then had to work a further six years to secure their release. While slave owners were compensated for their loss of earnings, most slaves received nothing. Freedom and equality were not immediately given to the descendants of African slaves.

Blacks, although free, were never treated equally and were often seen as inferior, sometimes as less than human. These views were held by many people for years. The truth is that such attitudes of superiority and inferiority take more than a generation to really change. During the mid-twentieth century, the struggle for freedom and equality for the descendants of African slaves continued. In the USA, the civil rights movement protested against the segregation of the races. In the UK, the *Windrush* generation (my parents' generation) became the early pioneers of multiracial Britain in the 1950s and 1960s. They were invited to a land of opportunity, to help rebuild the mother country after the Second World War. The harsh reality for many was low-income jobs, poor housing and racial abuse. It must be said that much progress has been made, both in the UK and the USA. In 2008 that progress was epitomized by Lewis Hamilton, when he became not only the youngest, but the first black Formula One winner. In the USA we celebrated the historic election of President Barack Obama to the White House. But for many people, our history still remains an unresolved issue.

Dr Don Carson, reflecting on racism and on the situation in America, said,

> On the one hand, there is [a] long-persisting and scarcely-admitted assumption among many, many non-African Americans that African Americans are inferior, along with some unvoiced assumptions that 'they' should grow up and get over it; and, on the other, there is a long-standing fear among African Americans that they just might be inferior, or, at least as bad, that other Americans might think them to be inferior, so that they can never measure up.

He went on to say, 'I once read about a boy who asked his father, "How come black people never do anything important?"'

I once heard a Christian woman say that she wouldn't give her children certain types of name, for fear that people might think they were black.

The brown-eyed, blue-eyed experiment

In 1968, the day after Martin Luther King was assassinated, Jane Elliott, a primary school teacher in Riceville, Iowa, USA, carried out an experiment on her third-grade pupils (eight-year-olds). Her purpose was to try to explain to them how Martin Luther King came to be shot, and also to show the effects of years of oppression, separation and segregation on people and their relationships. What she did has had a profound effect on the lives of thousands of people all over the world. Her powerful experiment demonstrates for us the legacy of the effects of prejudice, separation, rejection and oppression on people.

Jane Elliott divided her all-white third-grade students into two groups: one blue-eyed and one brown-eyed. She told the brown-eyed students they were smarter, nicer and cleaner, and deserved more privileges than the others. She told the blue-eyed students that they were inferior and not as clever as the brown-eyed students. What she discovered was amazing. Brown-eyed students became not only better behaved, but also more likely to learn. One dyslexic boy learnt how to read for the first time. The grades of clever blue-eyed children went down within hours of being told they were inferior. Friendships were torn apart and many of the brown-eyed children behaved arrogantly and aggressively towards the others, who became withdrawn, ashamed and angry. While I would in no way endorse the ethics of carrying out such an experiment on children, much can be learnt from the shocking effects on those involved.

Until 1984, Jane Elliott carried out her controversial experiment in her classroom. Since 1984, she has been carrying out her experiment in training contexts for companies and organizations all over the world. Other groups have also picked up on this experiment. In the UK, some schools have used this experiment in assemblies when trying to teach young people the effects of racism, discrimination and prejudice. The schools haven't used physical characteristics but red and green cards, which become symbols of difference. Negative attributes are assigned to cards of one colour, and positive attributes and privileges to cards of the other colour. The aim is to draw out three main points.

First, imagine that holding a green card means that you are superior to anyone holding a red card. What is the effect on people with green cards and red cards? Towards the end of 2006, a report published by the Department for Children, Schools and Families showed that Afro-Caribbean children in the UK are three times more likely to be excluded from school because of systematic racial discrimination. The report said that 'black pupils are disproportionately denied mainstream education and the life chances that go with it'. For some people, life can feel like being given a red card.

Secondly, what happens if your father, mother, grand-father and grandmother also had red cards? How would that affect you today? In his 'A More Perfect Union' speech, deliv-ered during his successful presidential campaign in 2008, Barack Obama, whose father was a Kenyan immigrant and his mother a white American, spoke, in response to issues of race being raised during his campaign, on the subject of the 'legacy of defeat black people have inherited':

> But for all those who scratched and clawed their way to get
> a piece of the American Dream, there were many who didn't
> make it – those who were ultimately defeated, in one way or
> another, by discrimination. That legacy of defeat was passed on
> to future generations.

Thirdly, how do people with green cards respond to the injustices they see being carried out on people with red cards? Jane Elliott conducted her experiment on the *Oprah Winfrey Show* in 1992. As the discussion moved towards racism, the audience said that they knew what was happen-ing was wrong, but they were afraid to stand up for what they knew was right.

Let's not walk away
These legacy issues surrounding history and race remain unresolved and complex and are often a source of tension. They are usually beneath the surface and rarely talked about openly. When they are, things can often become highly emotive very quickly, as many of these experiments have demonstrated. For the sake of peace, on the surface at least, these issues are ignored and people withdraw into the

security of their own groups. When they do come together, they focus on the positive aspects of diversity and avoid the more challenging aspects. Barack Obama also said,

> Race is an issue that I believe this nation cannot afford to ignore right now ... The fact is that the ... issues that have surfaced ... reflect the complexities of race in this country that we've never really worked through – a part of our union that we have yet to perfect. And if we walk away now, if we simply retreat into our respective corners, we will never be able to come together and solve challenges we face ...
>
> Understanding this reality requires a reminder of how we arrived at this point. As William Faulkner once wrote, 'The past isn't dead and buried. In fact, it isn't even past.'

The race issue in the USA may appear more overt and more easily linked to its history than in Britain, but in my view these comments can just as easily apply to the UK context. The race issue remains unresolved and it begins with the history and legacy. Yet in our relationships and the world today we have an opportunity to tackle this issue like never before. Let's not walk away and retreat into our own communities, as previous generations did. Let's not find clever ways of introducing modern segregation and separation, but rather let's come together to resolve and move on from our shared histories.

A biblical account of history

One of the most shocking stories Jesus ever told was that of the Good Samaritan (Luke 10:25–37). When we read about the Good Samaritan we think of its primary lessons as identifying one's neighbour and challenging some of our assumptions about people. It is about both of those things, but it also exposes even more deeply held views. It also exposes how history continues to impact on people many hundreds of years later.

The Samaritans were hated by the Jews, even though they were closely related. Historically, the Samaritans were made up of the remnant of the ten tribes of Israel and other peoples who were brought to Samaria by the king of Assyria (2 Kings 17:24) to replace the Israelites taken into exile in Assyria. The resident Israelites intermarried and mixed with this group. Over the years, Jews and Samaritans clashed and lived with genuine hostility towards one another. The Jews considered the Samaritans semi-foreign and semi-pagan. By Jesus' day, it was against Jewish law for Jews to mix with Samaritans (John 4:9) because they were considered ceremonially unclean. Why does that make it a shocking story? According to R. T. Kendall in *The Parables of Jesus*, the Good Samaritan is about pride and prejudice. The Jews were socially, racially, culturally and theologically prejudiced against the Samaritans. The idea that a Samaritan was the 'good guy' compared with a priest and a Levite would have been not only unthinkable but also offensive. No doubt when Jesus asked the expert in the law, 'Which was the neighbour to that man?' his reply came through gritted teeth! It is also about pride, in the sense that people don't like to give glory, honour and respect to someone who doesn't think, act or look like them; to someone who doesn't quite fit their idea of a hero or a good example. The Jews would probably have been happier if the story had focused on a Jewish good guy who helped a Samaritan.

The main point, though, is the history. The Jews and Samaritans had much negative history, which according to some scholars had lasted for centuries. Yet in Acts 1:8 Jesus says, 'You will be my witnesses in Jerusalem, and in all Judea and Samaria, and to the ends of the earth.' The gospel was not going to be bound and restricted, even by centuries of hostile relationships. If Jesus can command his first disciples to take the gospel across hostile divides, he can command us to reach across the divide.

The church's response

In many ways, the response of the church has been no different from that of societies around it, in that some churches appear as divided by race as other parts of the community. Trying to resolve race issues and understand history does not appear to have been a great priority for the church. Some churches are now seeking to address these challenges, but there is still much to be done. Bishop John Francis of Ruach Ministries, a large black-majority church in Brixton, expressed his desire for his church to become multicultural: 'Some people find it difficult to accept the way black people express themselves. However, if we take Christ's commands seriously, our churches must reflect the community.'

For all these challenges, the church has a potential that the world can only dream about. The Bible paints a picture of reconciliation across the divides that the church has not yet fully explored. The church's potential to bring people together, without the need for legislation and rules, because of the love displayed in Christ on the cross is quite staggering.

In the next chapter, we will begin to look at how we start to do this. We will see how God can help us deal with some of the issues surrounding our histories through repentance and forgiveness. We will see how we can seek reconciliation, which will help us to deal with our history, not by ignoring it and trying to forget it, but by facing it, resolving it, and moving on together in unity. This is what the church is called to do, both within itself and as an example to the world around us.

A prophetic picture

In the last days

the mountain of the LORD's temple will be established
    as chief among the mountains;
it will be raised above the hills,
    and all nations will stream to it.

Many peoples will come and say,

'Come, let us go to the mountain of the LORD . . .
He will teach us his ways,
    so that we may walk in his paths.'
(Isaiah 2:2–3)

Isaiah paints an amazing picture of the church at the forefront of reconciliation and bringing the nations together, to the point where others look on and come in order to find out for themselves what God is like. In this way, the church has a potential found nowhere else in society. No other religion or philosophy of life offers the same opportunity for unity in diversity as the church does. When nations come together across all sorts of barriers of history, race and stereotypes, the church does something no other group or society can dream of. But we don't only dream of it; God offers us the opportunity to experience it, because this is part of his great and glorious gospel. It may currently remain an untapped potential, but his people are beginning to dream and act.

Questions for discussion

How do you feel about your history? In what ways would you say your personal/cultural/racial history has affected your life?

Why do you think some people are so affected by their histories?

What can we learn from the story of the Good Samaritan about how people respond to history?

In what ways does the Isaiah passage relate to the church of today?

5. WHAT ABOUT ISSUES OF FORGIVENESS, REPENTANCE AND RECONCILIATION?

Learning to forgive

Everyday life is full of small apologies. But sometimes God calls us to go much deeper, as this moving extract from Corrie ten Boom's *The Hiding Place* shows:

It was in a church in Munich that I saw him, a balding heavy-set man in a gray overcoat, a brown felt hat clutched between his hands. People were filing out of the basement room where I had just spoken. It was 1947 and I had come from Holland to defeated Germany with the message that God forgives . . .

And that's when I saw him, working his way forward against the others. One moment I saw the overcoat and the brown hat; the next, a blue uniform and a visored cap with its skull and crossbones. It came back with a rush: the huge room with its harsh overhead lights, the pathetic pile of dresses and shoes in the center of the floor, the shame of walking naked past this man. I could see my sister's frail form ahead of me, ribs sharp beneath the parchment skin. Betsie, how thin you were!

Betsie and I had been arrested for concealing Jews in our home during the Nazi occupation of Holland; this man had been a guard at Ravensbruck concentration camp where we were sent ...

'You mentioned Ravensbruck in your talk,' he was saying. 'I was a guard in there.' No, he did not remember me. 'But since that time,' he went on, 'I have become a Christian. I know that God has forgiven me for the cruel things I did there, but I would like to hear it from your lips as well. Fräulein ...' his hand came out, '... will you forgive me?'

And I stood there – I whose sins had every day to be forgiven – and could not. Betsie had died in that place – could he erase her slow terrible death simply for the asking?

It could not have been many seconds that he stood there, hand held out, but to me it seemed hours as I wrestled with the most difficult thing I had ever had to do.

For I had to do it – I knew that. The message that God forgives has a prior condition: that we forgive those who have injured us. 'If you do not forgive men their trespasses,' Jesus says, 'neither will your Father in heaven forgive your trespasses.'

And still I stood there with the coldness clutching my heart. But forgiveness is not an emotion – I knew that too. Forgiveness is an act of the will, and the will can function regardless of the temperature of the heart. 'Jesus, help me!' I prayed silently. 'I can lift my hand, I can do that much. You supply the feeling.'

And so, woodenly, mechanically, I thrust my hand into the one stretched out to me. And as I did, an incredible thing took place. The current started in my shoulder, raced down my arm, sprang into our joined hands. And then this healing warmth seemed to flood my whole being, bringing tears to my eyes.

'I forgive you, brother!' I cried. 'With all my heart!'

For a long moment we grasped each other's hands, the former guard and the former prisoner. I had never known God's love so intensely as I did then.

A theology of forgiveness, repentance and reconciliation

There is not a lot written about the issues of forgiveness, repentance and reconciliation across the racial divide. Indeed, among all the books I have on the issue of race and diversity, there is only one that allocates two short chapters to the issue directly. Many such books seem to focus primarily on how we should value one another and work together. They tend only to touch on the issue of reconciliation between people across racial divides, without really addressing some of the fundamental issues. Yet there are two fundamental issues that can help us get to the point of reconciliation: namely repentance and forgiveness.

In the previous chapter I addressed issues surrounding history and legacy which remain unresolved for many people. Interestingly, in other situations of major conflict, repentance and forgiveness have been more openly addressed. Corrie ten Boom's moving account demonstrates that, within a couple of years of the Second World War, people on both sides of the conflict were speaking about forgiveness. In his powerful book *No Future Without Forgiveness*, Desmond Tutu also addresses the issue, directly relating it to some of the horrors of apartheid, through the Truth and Reconciliation Commission.

As diversity grows in our churches, so too does the need and opportunity to address issues from the past that continue to divide people. I recently did a study of Bible passages that made reference to forgiveness, repentance and reconciliation. It was quite revealing. There are around seventy references in the Bible to forgiveness. I found thirty that talk about repentance and fifteen that speak of reconciliation. I have outlined some of what I consider the key verses on these issues, and I have summarized the biblical position and what lessons we can learn from it.

Forgiveness

> But you are a forgiving God, gracious and compassionate, slow to anger and abounding in love.
> (Nehemiah 9:17)

> Jesus said, 'Father, forgive them, for they do not know what they are doing.'
> (Luke 23:34)

> Bear with each other and forgive whatever grievances you may have against one another. Forgive as the Lord forgave you.
> (Colossians 3:13)

God is a forgiving God. Forgiveness is one of the characteristics of God. Jesus, God's Son, showed the depth and strength of his character when he cried out in forgiveness on the cross. Sometimes forgiveness stands alone, particularly on those occasions when it is neither followed nor preceded by repentance. Forgiveness in these contexts requires the depth of character that Jesus displayed on the cross. Paul encourages the church to practise forgiveness just like Jesus did. This basic Christian value of forgiveness is not a one-off act but a continual process.

Lessons in true forgiveness from Philemon
The letter to Philemon in the New Testament is the story of a runaway slave called Onesimus, whom the apostle

Paul returned to his master. The word 'forgiveness' is not mentioned at all in the text, yet the book has some very clear lessons to offer on forgiveness. You may want to read the letter of Philemon before continuing with this chapter. It is short and should only take a few minutes.

Philemon is probably a leader in the church at Colossae which meets at his house. He is relatively wealthy and owns a number of slaves. One of them, a slave called Onesimus, has run away and taken things that belong to Philemon. He finds himself in Rome, where he meets the apostle Paul, who is in prison. There Onesimus becomes a Christian and experiences a dramatic change in his life. Paul is sending Onesimus back to Philemon, which is the right thing to do under the laws of that country. With him he sends a letter, appealing to Philemon to handle Onesimus in a Christian manner. According to the law of the land, Philemon owns Onesimus and can punish him very severely for running away.

I want to look at some lessons we can learn, when it comes to true forgiveness, from the short letter of Philemon. I will then give some practical pointers as to how we can move forward in this area and, hopefully, make progress.

Relationships are as important as doctrine

The book of Philemon shows us how Paul dealt with a complex and delicate relational matter and put into perspective the importance of right relationships. Some people believe that Christianity needs to change only what we believe: that is, our thoughts. This letter makes it clear that knowing Jesus means that we also need to change how we treat other people: that is, our words and attitudes.

The atrocities committed by Hutus and Tutsis against one another in Rwanda in 1994 were horrific and difficult to fathom. They are even more surprising when you realize that 90% of Rwanda's people are professing Christians. John D. Roth shares that an Inter-Varsity leader in the region explained: 'Missionaries preached a gospel about having a right relationship with God but not necessarily a right relationship with one another.'

At a practical level, true forgiveness ...

- *Can be tricky*

   'No longer as a slave, but better than a slave, as a dear brother' (Philemon 16).

   For Philemon to receive Onesimus back into his household was not as straightforward or simple as it may sound. Slaves were routinely punished for running away. Onesimus had been a troublesome slave. Paul describes him as being useless. It appears that he robbed his master and then ran away. What sort of message would not punishing Onesimus send to other slaves or slave owners? It would show Philemon to be weak, and he would lose face. Other slaves might think to themselves that becoming a Christian could automatically lead to further freedom and being treated like a brother.

   One of the other complexities in this story is the idea that a slave should seek the forgiveness of his master for running away. Why should the oppressed seek the forgiveness of his oppressor for trying to escape oppression? Even today, true forgiveness occurs in many different forms and can be tricky for a number of reasons:
   - The serious nature of the problem or the wrong committed;
   - The pain caused, and ongoing issues of pain and guilt (especially if the act or acts that have caused pain continue);

- The possible repercussions of offering forgiveness;
- A lack of acknowledgment from one of the parties
  of their need for forgiveness;
- Not always knowing who to forgive.

This is where the reality of Jesus' words bites home. How many times must I forgive my brother? Seventy times seven? Is that for every offence or in total? When it comes to handling pain, hurt and offence, what are you like? Are you like a vacuum cleaner (that keeps all the pain and hurt inside), or a dishwasher (which cleans it off and washes it away)? Our natural inclination is to disregard the obligation to forgive when it carries with it a high price in terms of our pride, humility and the desire for justice or vengeance.

- *Does not excuse sin*
  'If he has done you any wrong or owes you anything, charge it to me' (18).

  Paul did not dismiss the possible offences committed by Onesimus. In fact he offered to pay for any wrong he might have done. True forgiveness does not forget wrongdoing or try to diminish it or sweep it under the carpet, or even rationalize or justify it. True forgiveness must face the sin and the anger, the hurt and the pain. At the cross, Jesus took our sin. It is here that we find true and ultimate forgiveness. Whether we are slaves or free in this life, in Christ we can know true freedom. The Christian message does not place us neatly as either victims or perpetrators; but we are all slaves to sin and caught in a web of sin, and we all require his grace and forgiveness to free us from that.
- *Is motivated by love, not duty*
  'I appeal to you on the basis of love' (9).

Paul asked Philemon to act out of love, not duty.
Paul had high expectations that Philemon would not
simply respond in a dutiful Christian way, but rather
out of love. We must also learn to forgive because
of love, not duty. Just as the Corrie Ten Boom story
shows, sometimes a small step of forgiveness as an act
of the will is met by God rushing in to confirm it in our
heart and enable that act to become a genuine one.

- *Is a deep and meaningful act*

'He is very dear to me but even dearer to you, both
as a man and as a brother' (16).

In today's world, forgiveness can be a trivial act.
We glibly say, 'I beg your pardon; please forgive me';
'All's well that ends well'; and 'let bygones be bygones'.
These are all meaningless clichés that have very little
to do with real forgiveness. Much of the language
associated with forgiveness has become associated
with mere common politeness, causing it to lose much
of its deeper meaning. Mixed with Philemon's anger
towards Onesimus' actions may also have been some
disappointment, pain and hurt. Forgiveness was going
to have to be deep, real and intentional. We have to
be careful that when we approach God and ask for
forgiveness, we do not make that a superficial request,
but a genuinely heartfelt one.

- *Is about restoration, not revenge*

'I am sending him – who is my very heart – back to
you' (12).

The whole aim of this letter is restoration rather
than retribution and revenge. This is true Christian
forgiveness. True forgiveness brings healing in
relationships, not division. The following is an extract
from Desmond Tutu's *No Future Without Forgiveness*.

It is the true story of the abduction and murder of Marietta Jaeger's seven-year-old daughter, while she and her family were on holiday in Montana, USA. Marietta describes her experience after the murderer had been arrested.

> I had finally come to believe that real justice is not punishment but restoration, not necessarily to how things used to be, but to how they really should be. In both the Hebrew and Christian scriptures whence my beliefs come, the God who rises up from them is a God of mercy and compassion, a God who seeks not to punish, destroy, or put us to death, but a God who works unceasingly to help and heal us, rehabilitate and reconcile us, restore us to the richness and fullness of life for which we have been created. This, now, was the justice I wanted for this man who had taken my little girl.

After the killer of her daughter was arrested, Marietta eventually met him and was able to forgive him.

- *Sets us free from the past*

 'Formerly he was useless to you, but now he has become useful both to you and to me' (11).

Onesimus had come to faith in Christ and this set him free from the past, a past which had included theft and running away from his responsibilities. Now he finds himself helping the apostle and living up to his name, which actually means 'useful'. God's forgiveness sets us free. Onesimus can now come back to Philemon with a clean slate.

Repentance

Therefore this is what the LORD says: 'If you repent, I will restore you that you may serve me.'
(Jeremiah 15:19)

If your brother sins, rebuke him, and if he repents, forgive him.
(Luke 17:3)

Godly sorrow brings repentance that leads to salvation and leaves no regret.
(2 Corinthians 7:10)

We often think of repentance only as being related to initial salvation, a past act when in repentance and faith we came into a relationship with God. But repentance has a far greater meaning than that. Repentance is also linked to restoration, both in terms of our relationship with God, and also our relationships with other people. True repentance is the underlying key to living without regrets, finding restoration and serving God.

The following personal story is a real example of repentance. Donovan and Rhoda Walker attended a John Wimber conference on healing sometime around 1993:

When the sermon by John Wimber had concluded, we
were asked if there was anything or any person that we had
not forgiven before the Lord; the context of healing being
[sometimes] linked to forgiveness.

As we were walking out of the auditorium, we were
approached by a middle-aged white lady who tapped me
(Donovan) on the shoulder and asked if we had a minute to talk,
which we did. She explained that during the sermon she had

been convicted by the Holy Spirit that she had un-forgiveness towards Black people as a result of some previous issues that she didn't go into detail over. We were the first Black people that she could find, and she asked that we would receive her forgiveness for her hatred of Black people and ask that we pray for her.

We were more than happy to sit down with her, pray, and ask the Lord for forgiveness and healing. She felt delivered and set free. The whole experience was also very uplifting for Rhoda and me. Praise be to God.

Reconciliation

Therefore, if you are offering your gift at the altar and there remember that your brother has something against you, leave your gift there in front of the altar. First go and be reconciled to your brother.
(Matthew 5:23–24)

God was reconciling the world to himself in Christ, not counting men's sins against them. And he has committed to us the message of reconciliation.
(2 Corinthians 5:19)

But now he has reconciled you by Christ's physical body through death to present you holy in his sight.
(Colossians 1:22)

God's ultimate goal is reconciliation. To reconcile to himself all things, he has given us the task of taking this message of reconciliation to the world. Reconciliation is part of the Christian's mandate. The church should be setting the best examples of reconciliation as ambassadors of the God who reconciles. Reconciliation is the first step towards unity. When thinking through the issues of forgiveness and repentance, we must not lose sight of their purpose: reconciliation. Without forgiveness, repentance and reconciliation there can be no unity.

Reconciliation requires that we step towards our brothers and sisters, who may be hurt and in pain from things in the past, with love and acceptance. Reconciliation treats the relationship as primary, not the issues that bring pain and division. Though we may not fully understand it, for some people 'getting over the past and moving on' is not easy, and sometimes they need help to deal with past hurts and relationship breakdown. The challenge is not just for those who need to forgive, but for all of us to work together towards true reconciliation. The church ought to be setting an example in its dealing with negative histories, reaching across the divides to honour and accept people who are different from us. The church has a unique role in bringing reconciliation across the divides. I would go further and say the Christian gospel stands alone in its application of these key values of forgiveness, repentance and reconciliation.

How then does the church move forward as a community desiring diversity in unity, displaying something of God's amazing grace and manifold wisdom?

A particular issue

I don't want to raise issues that are not there or make more of issues than I need to, but there does seem to be a particular issue between black and white people which remains unresolved and requires forgiveness, repentance and reconciliation. This feels a bit strange to say, because where these relationships work well, they work very well, and I am also aware of huge progress that has been made. However, I am all too well aware of the unsaid and under-the-surface tensions and dynamics that can occur, even in good relationships. It may not be an issue in the same way as for other types of diversity, but I feel I need to address it.

The truth is that forgiveness and trust remain major hurdles for some black people. Some feel the pain of racism and a negative history, and live with feelings of resentment and bitterness which impact on their everyday relationships and attitudes. Black people, maybe more than others, are very sensitized to their history. You see, the published history of black people could be summed up in one word: rejection. This is the feeling of not being wanted or accepted as a race and never having achieved anything significant. In recent years, through events like Black History Month, there has been an attempt to redress an imbalance in how this history has been portrayed and to outline the significant contributions black people have made to the world around us. Rejection, however, is not just a whole-race problem, but the reality of many black people's personal experience.

In communities and churches across this country, as black people have moved into areas and joined churches, white people have moved out. This has happened so frequently that it has even been given a name: 'white flight'. There is (and in some ways this is understandable) a feeling among some whites in the UK of what can only be described as loss. The speed of growth among minority groups in the UK appears staggering. A sense of the loss of the way life and community that operated a few years ago is a real issue among many whites. This sense of loss is not wrong in itself. It is the reality of losing something that was dear to you. The fact is that some of what has been lost cannot be replaced, but other parts can be. That sense of a loss of what we might call 'national identity' can sometimes be expressed as, 'They are taking over.' The reality is that the vast majority of black and ethnic minority groups are not trying to take over. But they *are* trying to join in. When white people leave areas that have become diverse, it repeats a cycle that has been recurring for years and which can be summed up in this phrase: 'You can take over, but you can't join in.' For true integration to take place, this 'white flight' has to end – not just in our streets, but also in our churches. For the sake of the gospel that really promotes diversity in unity, this must happen.

So there are three challenges we face:

The challenge of forgiveness
Some of us need to learn the secret of true forgiveness. We need to face up to our hurts and pain, and forgive those who have wronged us. Some of us need to stop using our hurt and pain to hold people in bondage to shame and guilt, but rather to use the power of forgiveness to release them into freedom, liberty and relationship.

The challenge of repentance
Others of us need to repent of attitudes and prejudices that we have held. Often we may even be unaware that these attitudes exist within us until we come into close contact with people who are different. When we do become aware of these attitudes, we need to turn away from them. We need to repent.

The challenge of reconciliation
We all need to face the challenge of true reconciliation. Forgiveness and repentance take one person, but reconciliation takes two people. A community can forgive, but it requires two communities to be reconciled. It requires that we are in relationship and not withdrawing into our own

communities. For people to understand the true potential of the gospel of Christ, reconciliation must be sought. This is racial, social and cultural reconciliation.

How do we demonstrate that we have forgiven and repented, and are seeking reconciliation? By reaching out and pursuing true and genuine friendship across the divides. In this way, people will feel valued and accepted. These are some of the best antidotes to the hurt, pain and guilt of the past.

In the church of Jesus Christ there are no longer a 'them' and an 'us'. There are only us. I believe this is the way in which God wants his church of the future to operate. It will be a highly attractive community that people will want to follow and become a part of. A generation must emerge that champions and pursues true reconciliation across the divides. Let our generation be the one!

Questions for discussion
Whom do you need to forgive?

From whom do you need to seek forgiveness?

With whom do you need to seek reconciliation across the divide?

In what ways are you affected by wrongs of the past that touch other people's lives more than your own? How can you show more empathy?

6. WHY SHOULD WE CROSS THE DIVIDE IN RELATIONSHIPS AND WHAT ARE THE BENEFITS?

Helen's journal entry during the 'Gracism' series at King's Church, Catford:

3 March
11.12 pm

Someone said this evening that they are less than comfortable with the idea of being intentional about making cross-cultural friendships. As if somehow they were only doing it because they felt they had to, rather than it being natural. I can understand what they mean – how would I feel if someone was reaching out to me because they felt they had to, rather than from a genuine desire to get to know me? It would be hard to respond naturally to them. It is equally hard to be natural if one is under a compulsion. Yet someone, somehow, has to take the first step and reach out and maybe it will start out a little stiff and awkward but in the end we will find we can be friends in truth.

Conversations like this make me think we are really still just at the beginning and have much further to go than we think.

This chapter begins with two questions: 'Why do I need to cross the divide in relationships?' and 'What are the benefits?' At this point in the journey, the answers to these questions may seem somewhat self-explanatory. Isn't it obvious that we need to develop relationships across the divide? As people join our churches, what else would we want to do but reach out to them in love, acceptance and friendship? The journal entry above indicates that this desire to reach out is not necessarily something people always experience. I believe there are three important reasons why we should be asking these questions, and I want to spend some time unpacking them.

First, some people are genuinely asking these questions. 'I live in a diverse society and attend a diverse church. Isn't that enough? Why do I actually need to build relationships with people in other cultures, races, age ranges or different social contexts? What is wrong with my friends being like me?'

Secondly, most people gravitate and are drawn to people like themselves. Developing relationships with people from other races can seem quite an unnatural thing to do. Why then is it so important?

Thirdly, as we encourage one another to build relationships with people who are different from us, some people will feel led to attempt this because they feel they must, rather than because they want to. How do we respond to this? Is it right? Are there deeper reasons for reaching across the divide and greater rewards than just knowing we've 'done our duty'?

The first step to reaching across the divide is understanding why we need to do it. As we understand the rationale, it becomes easier to make the first step, and we experience a greater resolve to persevere when things get difficult or awkward. In this chapter we will look at some biblical and some practical reasons for building relationships across the divide. Alongside these, we will also explore some of the benefits and some of the challenges.

Jesus crossed the divide

In his death, Jesus crossed the ultimate divide for us, to bring us into relationship with God. In his life, he was the greatest example of one who crossed the divides. The truth is that we often focus on the spiritual side of Jesus' encounters with ordinary people, but there was also a very human side to these encounters, in which race, culture and gender played a huge part. For example, we talk of the faith of the Phoenician woman (Mark 7:25–30) without giving due regard to the cross-cultural nature of their encounter. A Phoenician woman, Greek-born and addressing a Jewish religious teacher and comparing herself with a dog! Here was someone who would have been considered the lowest of the low by the Jews. This encounter does not simply represent faith, but it also addresses issues of status and gender head on. It gives us a small insight into the type of world in which Jesus was ministering: a world where status, name, religion, class and race all played a major part in whom you spoke to, helped and called your friends. Jesus was clear that his earthly ministry was primarily to the Jews, yet his willingness to cross the divide and encounter different people and groups was high. His is an example we are encouraged to follow.

Furthermore, Jesus broke all the rules when it came to relationships and to both cultural and religious taboos. He healed lepers (Matthew 11:5) and mixed with outcasts such as tax collectors and sinners (Matthew 11:19). He exposed the motives of the rich and influential (Luke 12:16), and affirmed the actions of the poor (Luke 21:3). He changed the life of a Samaritan woman whom he met at a well (John 4). He encouraged people to love their enemies and do good to those who persecuted them (Matthew 5:44). As we read the gospel in the twenty-first century, it can be easy for us to miss some of the relational and social dynamics Jesus would have had to deal with on an almost daily basis. Yet he called his disciples to be with him, to be together and to serve one another. He finally commissioned them to go and make disciples of all nations (Matthew 28:19). In short, Jesus taught that the good news of the gospel was more than a cultural message, but radically crossed all 'uncrossable' boundaries and divides and brought people together.

It can take time for us to realize what an example Jesus gave us, and how we are to follow that example. Below are Gemma's and Dan's stories about how they have tried to follow Jesus' example in their small group.

Gemma

I've only known what it's like to be in the majority. Diversity and difference have been concepts that I've been exposed to, but they haven't affected me directly. My mother died when I was seven and from that age we always had au pairs in the house to look after my sister and me. They were from all over Europe: France, Germany, Italy, Spain, and even Croatia, during the Yugoslav war. For them, living in a strange country with a dysfunctional family must have been very different! But for me, it just meant I had to eat weird food and survive driving round roundabouts the wrong way! Difference is something my family are also used to, as my father's side are Jewish. They lived through the World Wars and, due to the level of anti-Semitism in this country, they decided to change their name from Cohen to Coleman.

So I've been an onlooker when it comes to diversity, but have never really thought that it was an issue that affected me or that I could contribute to, until Dan and I joined King's in 2005. It has become increasingly clear to me that, because I'm in the majority, diversity should be an issue that shapes my thoughts and actions if I'm going to follow Jesus' example.

Dan

A year after we joined King's, Gemma and I started to lead a small group which was born out of an Alpha Plus group (Alpha Plus being a follow-on course from Alpha). This meant that it was a group of people who were thrown together in a way, not a group of people that looked like us, had grown up in a similar environment, had the same experiences, or that we would naturally have clicked with. Our group is really diverse. We have members from their twenties into their sixties, who come from, or whose families come from, Jamaica, Nigeria, Tobago, St Lucia, Germany, and Togo. We have young couples, lone parents, teachers, social workers and everything in between.

This was a real challenge to begin with, as not only were we new to leading a group, but we were also new to building relationships with such a mixture of people. What we found over the weeks and months and now years, is that it really is God's plan for us to be family with *everyone* and that he gives the love for us to love others with. It's been he who has bound us together into real relationship with one another. We've had so much fun getting to know one another and finding out more about one another's backgrounds. One very funny evening we decided to get out the atlas to find out where Togo was!

We found that by recognizing our differences and discussing them, we all feel unique, special, and can learn more about one another. We've really enjoyed eating together (usually in Nandos!). By meeting in one another's houses we've got closer to one another, through seeing pictures of family, what books we have, paintings on the wall etc.

We're still learning so much about difference and diversity, but we really feel it has enriched us and is helping us to mature into the people God is calling us to be. We'd like to see Jesus' perfect example of inclusivity worked out practically in all small groups.

Reaching across the divide ...

Is an outworking of Jesus' death on the cross

> For he himself is our peace, who has made the two one and has destroyed the barrier, the dividing wall of hostility ... His purpose was to create in himself one new man out of the two, thus making peace, and in this one body to reconcile both of them to God through the cross, by which he put to death their hostility. (Ephesians 2:14–16)

God removed the barrier that existed not only between us and God, but between us and other people. The work of the cross was not just about my individual relationship with God being restored, but also about my relationship with my fellow man. As John Piper says, reconciliation across the divides is 'a blood of Jesus issue'. The cross has removed the barriers that exist between people. Jesus didn't break down the wall so that we could say 'Hi' across the divide and continue to live with barriers and walls between us. He broke down the wall and brought people together and made us family, fellow-citizens, members of his household. He removed the barriers so that we might love and serve one another as he encouraged his disciples to do; so that we might be one, just as he is one; and so the world may know he came from God. He has truly given us something to celebrate.

The gospel of Jesus has always had the potential to make friends out of enemies, fellow-citizens out of aliens, sons and daughters out of orphans. It has always had the power to bring the extremes together: Jew and Gentile, rich and poor, Palestinian and Jew, and young and old. As Bruce Milne says, in *Dynamic Diversity*, 'In his death Christ does things.' The first person I heard speak openly about this was a pastor who led a large multicultural church in Cape Town, South Africa, called Simon Petit. Using the book of Ephesians, he would preach about there being one new man/humanity in Christ. I began to realize that my 'hunch' that we should somehow all be together was in fact exactly what God had intended, and that he had made provision for it at the cross.

I had the privilege of attending a small group in Cape Town one evening. The first thing you noticed was the diversity: wealthy and poor, black and white. At least three or four different national languages were spoken by the group, including Afrikaans, English, Xhosa and Zulu. We joined in as the people worshipped, prayed and studied the Bible together in an atmosphere of humble gratitude for what God had done. Studying the Scriptures together helps to strengthen bonds and develop common ground with people, as we seek to learn from God's word. For me, it represented another perspective on the work of the cross. That small group was a very moving glimpse of the power of the cross to reconcile across the divide and bring both peace and restored relationships.

In *The Message of the Cross*, Derek Tidball writes:

Authentic reconciliation on the vertical dimension, with God, will result in genuine reconciliation on the horizontal dimension with one another. The church must not only preach the message of reconciliation, but also model it in its relationships.

Is part of God's ultimate plan

> After this I looked and there before me was a great multitude
> that no-one could count, from every nation, tribe, people and
> language, standing before the throne and in front of the Lamb ...
> And they cried out in a loud voice:
>
> > 'Salvation belongs to our God,
> > who sits on the throne,
> > and to the Lamb.'
> (Revelation 7:9–10)

God's ultimate plan is the reconciliation of all things to himself.
When Jesus taught his disciples to pray, he taught them to
pray, 'Your will be done on earth as it is in heaven.' In heaven
we find this diverse community of believers worshipping the
risen Lord Jesus. While church, as we know it, does not always
look like that, I believe it should at least be our aspiration to
replicate a glimpse of the heavenly community here on earth.

Feels more complete

Together with my family, I have attended many excellent
churches over the years. In fact, my wife and I have always
made a point of taking our girls to churches very different
from the one they are used to, with the aim of giving them
a broader perspective on the church. We have attended
churches that were bigger, smaller, predominately with young
or old people, churches on local estates and churches in leafy
suburbs. My observation from this experience is that churches
that have a good level of diversity can feel more complete and
more inclusive. An older white lady who attends a large urban
multicultural church has said to me on more than one occasion, 'When I visit churches that have little or no diversity, it
feels as though half the family is missing.'

Has mission benefit

My kids attended a local primary school which is very
diverse. In the past, the school asked parents to complete
questionnaires which focused on various aspects of school
life. Although there have never been any specific questions
relating to the cultural make-up of the school, many parents
have, unprompted, made positive comments about the fact
that it is diverse. At King's Church, we sometimes used questionnaires on the streets as a way of opening up discussions
and sharing the gospel. In the past, when we questioned
people on the streets about the area they lived in, many of
them would say that diversity is a positive. That is also a
comment made by new people who visited the church. We
live in a world where, for all the tensions diversity can create,
many people see it as a positive. These are from different
backgrounds and races and different ages. Some of those
most positive about diversity in King's Church are between
the ages of sixty and ninety, mainly white and female! For all
the complexities of diversity in church, it can be seen as a real
evangelistic tool for reaching out to different people, and to
both new and existing communities. I heard of one family
who joined a local multicultural church. One of the reasons
they gave for joining was, 'We can now bring to church the
friends we have who are not like us.'

Our society has grappled for years with the tensions created
when different communities live together. Imagine for a
moment having churches all over the world in which people
who naturally did not mix, and in fact were often hostile to
one another, came together to worship God and express
genuine Christian love and friendship with one another.

A friend of mine tells the story of going to sleep each night
counting the bombs going off in his home town in Northern
Ireland. He describes a life during 'The Troubles' of complete

religious segregation between Protestants and Catholics. He then talks of the time when he became a Christian, and of how he was able to reach across the divide to an Irish Catholic whom he met while studying for his degree in London. He describes how this man became one of his closest friends.

Imagine if the church truly woke up to the fact that the gospel really does have the power to reconcile people across the divides: that Jesus really meant us to break down barriers and that he had really removed the tensions and hostilities between people. Just imagine what the world would make of that! And it does not need to be something only for our imaginations. Because of the gospel, people are reaching across the divides and being reconciled.

Helps us appreciate our differences and alleviate our tensions

If you are from a minority group, you will already know that there are at least two ways of seeing and doing things. There is the way of the majority of this nation, and then there is your own ethnic or minority group way. If you are part of the majority, you won't necessarily know that. This realization comes as we get to know one another.

When we reach across the divide, we develop a greater understanding of people and their cultures, and why people do things in the way that they do. This can alleviate tension and misunderstanding and can even be enriching and fun, as Gemma's and Dan's accounts of their small-group experience illustrates.

Brings new confidence

Taking some initial steps to reach out across the cultural divide brings confidence when dealing with new situations and new cultures. My wife told me recently of how, in her

work, she was playing the tune 'Auld Lang Syne' on the piano.
This led to a discussion with a Shona-speaking Zimbabwean
woman. My wife had the confidence to pursue a conversation with this woman and discovered that the tune of 'Auld
Lang Syne' was sung in Zimbabwe at funerals. She was able
to describe how the song was used in this country on New
Year's Eve, to welcome in the New Year. Each had learnt
something new about the other's experience. Starting with
small steps like this, we build our confidence as we attempt
to grow relationships with people whose backgrounds are
different from our own.

Helps in overcoming negative stereotypes

I don't know about you, but I find that, if I'm not careful,
I can, quite easily and almost without knowing it, develop
negative stereotypes. I may see a trait I consider to be negative in only a few people, but I can then very easily translate
it as being applicable to a whole group or community.

Here's a common one: 'Black people are always late.' We
may have observed this trait only in one or two people, but
we see it as a trait in the whole community. This can be the
case if we do not know many people from that community.
But when people like us are late, that's different, and we may
see that as just a trait of individual personality. Developing
friendships across the divide helps me to see people as individuals, and to resist the temptation to develop those negative
stereotypes which can so easily act as a barrier to building an
inclusive church and an inclusive society. This is one of the
greatest benefits of crossing the divide in relationships.

Makes us rich and keeps us humble

Diversity brings with it a richness of experience and learning. It brings a deeper appreciation of God and the work of

the cross. It keeps us humble when we realize that there are many very legitimate ways of doing and seeing things that are different from ours: perhaps even *better* ways of doing certain things. We no longer think of our way as always being right. The universal message of the cross kills ethnocentric thinking and helps us to identify the blind spots we can often develop for the flaws in our own culture!

Helps us to reach out to people from other religions
The Christian message of forgiveness and reconciliation applies to our relationships with both God and our fellow people, and this sets the Christian faith apart. No other faith has this potential or makes the offer of reconciliation with other people in the way that the Christian faith does. Reaching across the divide in relationships is a key aspect of this.

So why don't we reach across the divide in relationships?
We have looked at the reasons why we ought to cross the divide, and the benefits of doing so. Let's look briefly at some of the things we should be aware of that can hinder us in reaching out. They are often very simple.

Time
All relationships take time to develop. Genuine relationships do not develop overnight, even with those people with whom we may find we have an immediate chemistry and connection. They take time. Relationships that develop too quickly often do not have enough to sustain them when they go through difficult patches, as most relationships eventually do. The truth is that relationships across the divide are no different, and can take even longer to develop. The possibility of misunderstanding and confusion is much greater. Imagine

inviting your new Zimbabwean friends over for your New Year's Eve party, in which you all join hands and loudly sing 'Auld Lang Syne'! It could lead to an interesting conversation! Many of us feel we just don't have the time to develop such relationships.

Effort

It requires effort. Some friendships come more easily than others. Often it is much easier to develop relationships with people just like us. It would be fair to say that many of the friendships my wife and I value and maintain are with couples similar to us, in that, like us, they are in mixed-race relationships. There can sometimes be an immediate connection with other couples who have crossed the divide in their marriages. However, we are also intentional in reaching out to people who are different from us, whether in racial background, marital status or whatever. These relationships do sometimes take a little more effort and time to develop, but they are always worth it.

Fear

One church member wrote in his personal journal:

> This is one I'm keen to break, one emotion that I have felt quite a lot if I'm honest: fear. After thinking about it, I tend to panic quite easily and often end up being slightly fearful that I would be viewed as completely ignorant, rude, exclusive and, worst of all, racist or prejudiced. I'm certain this one comes into relational aspects as well.

We can be fearful of stepping outside our comfort zones and reaching out to people who are different. Fear can often arise from not understanding different cultures, and therefore we can feel unable to deal with things that come up. In addition, we may be afraid of saying the wrong thing and being thought of as ignorant. This may be related to a desire not to offend someone by saying the wrong thing. It may also be a fear of trusting people, because you have been there before, made yourself vulnerable, and been hurt or felt exposed by someone's reaction. It can also be a fear of being judged by others.

To sum up ...

When we take steps to cross the divide, God uses these encounters to make us rich and keep us humble. Such encounters offer a challenge and a hope to the world: a challenge in that people are impressed when the church is able to demonstrate such unity, but also hope that diversity can be made to work in such a positive way.

Finally, it just makes sense of who God is and what he has done. It follows the example of the Lord Jesus and enriches our worship of him, and brings more glory and honour to his name. Hallelujah!

Questions for discussion

What experience have you had of building relationships across the divide?

Jesus crossed the divide. How does knowing that motivate you to do the same?

Can you think of other reasons, in addition to mine, why people don't reach across the divide?

Of all the reasons for crossing the divide, which appeal to you the most?

7. HOW DO I DEVELOP RELATIONSHIPS ACROSS THE DIVIDE?

The elf and the dwarf

I am a huge fan of the excellent film trilogy based on the epic novel *The Lord of the Rings* by J. R. R. Tolkien. On one occasion, I watched all three extended movies in one day!

In the first film, *The Fellowship of the Ring*, Gimli, son of Gloin (a dwarf), and Legolas (an elf) develop an unusual friendship. Their first encounter at the Fellowship of the Ring is one of suspicion and some hostility. With lots of negative history and bad blood between the elves and the dwarves, it isn't long before this surfaces between them. However, over time they develop a strong bond as they play their part in the story of *The Lord of the Rings*. Both feel committed and connected to another important character in the film – Aragorn, son of Arathorn – and it is this common purpose that brings them together. They risk their lives for each other and introduce each other to parts of their histories and backgrounds. For me, it becomes one of the many endearing parts of the film: an unusual relationship between an elf and a dwarf, based on shared experiences, a common mission and a growing mutual respect.

Many of my closest friendships have developed while doing things with someone else, and a common activity has really helped when crossing the divide in my relationships: anything from travelling as part of a team taking aid to Romania, volunteering to help at a large youth event, or helping out regularly on the church welcome team. Each becomes a shared experience with a common purpose, and mutual respect grows as you learn to appreciate one another's gifts and talents.

One of the most common questions I have been asked on the issue of diversity by people in my church is this: 'Why do we keep talking about diversity when we are already diverse?' This is a valid question. If you are in a church which is already drawing people from very different backgrounds and cultures, why the need to talk about it and spend time addressing it? Surely we don't need to talk about it if it's happening already. However, if we want to build churches that are not only diverse at a congregational level, but also in leadership, diverse in personal relationships, diverse in worship and in practical ministries, we continually have to examine the way we are building. Developing and integrating diversity, like many things, is a process of change. Understanding where you are at in that process can help you manage your own and others' expectations. Begin from where you are. Be a learner. Pray, ask questions and act.

Levels of diversity

Let's look together at some of the different levels of diversity. As the chapter progresses, we will explore how we can develop relationships that will go deeper and deeper.

Facilitating – the congregation

Jesus always had a diverse congregation in mind. The church congregation is the place that begins to facilitate diversity. Until recently, church congregations rarely became diverse intentionally. People from a minority group tended to join an existing church which would begin to make room for them. However, in more recent times, new churches have been planted, particularly in cities and large urban areas, where the people have had an expressed desire to become a diverse community.

Congregations are the first level at which diverse relationships become possible in church. At this level, relationships are often positive but still fairly superficial: you don't necessarily know someone's name. You say 'Hello' on a Sunday and enjoy a warm, albeit quite superficial, conversation. Many relationships begin here and develop, although some people are content for their relationships to remain at this level. Churches can encourage relationships by creating more social time around the service: for example, by taking a break in the middle or at the end of the meeting.

Fellowship – the small group

In my church experience, small groups have always been important: meetings of around eight to twelve people in someone's home, usually for worship, discussion of the Sunday sermon, or Bible study and prayer. Their purpose is to take relationships a bit deeper and to replicate something of what we read about in Acts 2:46, where people met together in one another's homes. As my church has grown, the importance of small groups has increased. Actually getting into small groups can be the first hurdle for minority groups coming into the church. However, from the perspective of personal relationships, small groups represent the next level.

At this level, people have the opportunity to get to know someone personally. Meeting in someone's home is naturally less formal than a Sunday service. As in the congregation, relationships are likely to be positive. Differences might become a bit more obvious, but are not necessarily discussed. Again, some people are content for relationships to remain at this level, confined if you like to the small group meeting rather than becoming more personal. But the small group at least creates the potential for relationships to go deeper, a possibility which might not have been there otherwise.

Friendship – the meal

At this point, we begin to engage with diversity at a slightly deeper level. We don't just say 'Hello' like acquaintances. I don't just know your name and what you do for a living, but I am beginning to get to know you. Differences can become more obvious, though we may sometimes struggle to distinguish between what may be cultural and personality differences. The truth is that it can so often be a mixture of both. This level can lead to genuine friendships that develop and go deeper. But it can also require more effort and a degree of vulnerability, and there is therefore a danger that we may hold back.

This is a key level, which I now want us to explore in a bit more detail. In Acts 11 and Galatians 2, Peter gives us one of the foundational ways we can cross the divide, which is eating together. This is sometimes referred to as table fellowship. Peter is criticized when he engages in it and criticized when he doesn't. Why did table fellowship lead to such a reaction?

'So when Peter went up to Jerusalem, the circumcised believers criticised him and said, "You went into the house of uncircumcised men and ate with them"' (Acts 11:2–3).

The outpouring of the Spirit in Caesarea, which led to the first true Gentile converts (aside from the Ethiopian eunuch), was first greeted by the Jewish believers with criticism. Their criticism was directed at the actions of Peter. Peter ate with the Gentiles, something which Jewish law forbade. He ate with people who were uncircumcised. Jewish Christians still held on tightly to the cultural baggage of food laws and circumcision. It was only in the face of such a development as the progress of the gospel to the Gentiles that their cultural expectations were suddenly being challenged. This phenomenon of eating together became a powerful sign of the work of the gospel – people who were once far from one another, separated by religion, tradition and culture, now ate together.

> When Peter came to Antioch, I opposed him to his face, because he was clearly in the wrong. Before certain men came from James, he used to eat with the Gentiles. But when they arrived, he began to draw back and separate himself from the Gentiles because he was afraid of those who belonged to the circumcision group. The other Jews joined him in his hypocrisy, so that by their hypocrisy even Barnabas was led astray.
>
> When I saw that they were not acting in line with the truth of the gospel, I said to Peter in front of them all, 'You are a Jew, yet you live like a Gentile and not like a Jew. How is it, then, that you force Gentiles to follow Jewish customs?'
> (Galatians 2:11–13)

In this second passage, Paul opposes Peter to his face because he was in the wrong. Once again the issue is around food. This time Peter withdraws from eating with the Gentiles. His actions are seen as being out of step with the gospel. The gospel had broken down cultural barriers and enabled people to come together. Paul saw Peter's withdrawal as a potential denial of something the cross had achieved and a replacement of the barriers the cross had removed. Paul's passion for what Christ had achieved comes to the fore.

In some ways, what, how, where, when and with whom we eat expresses our culture as nothing else does. Some people may prefer to eat sitting on the floor or using their hands. Others may use sticks or other utensils. Some prefer to eat in large family groups, while others sit apart from family members. Eating is one of the most natural expressions of our cultures. People very rarely eat with people not like themselves, except perhaps in a fast food restaurant! So, in this most cultural and intimate of activities, governed by religion, tradition and race, God makes a profound change, right there. The barriers of division are broken down, and a sign of this is eating together: Christians can eat together across the divide.

The two occasions on which Peter received criticism were first, when he ate with some people; and secondly, because he stopped eating with some other people. Eating was a hugely symbolic sign for the circumcised, in keeping them separate as God's chosen people; but also for the Christian, in demonstrating what the cross of Christ had done in reconciling them, not only to God but to others.

So how do we apply this truth today? Jesus left us with a powerfully symbolic meal that we are to share with other believers until he returns. Taking part in the communion meal and acknowledging not only what Christ has done for us as individuals, but also the unity he has brought to us in the midst of all our diversity, is a reminder that he has made it possible for us to cross the divide. The importance of eating together says something not only about our faith, but also about our relationships.

Different cultures and families have different approaches to hospitality. I grew up in a family where there was always room for one more. I remember one occasion when my brother, sisters and I brought home a number of friends for dinner one Sunday after church. My mum, whom you met in chapter one, made sure that the food stretched, a bit like the loaves and fishes! She would also get people involved in helping her prepare dinner. On the other hand, while dating my wife Pauline, I had to let her know at lunchtime the day before if I was coming for tea. Her parents would serve their guests and you wouldn't be expected to help out in any way (I quite liked that!). Both families were very hospitable but had very different ways of expressing their hospitality.

So the meal becomes a crucial level in helping to understand our differences and develop friendships across the divide.

Freedom – the story

At this level, the relationship is such that sharing your story becomes more possible. We can all recount our experiences of diversity and difference as we were growing up, or for some of us our lack of experience of these things. For some of us, it will be true to say that we were unaware of how diversity and difference affect people. Others of us will have been aware from a young age that we were different and known the impact that can have. The point is that we all have stories to tell in which we can learn from one another and deepen our relationships; and, as the friendship deepens, we become more open.

During our 'Gracism' series at King's Church, we wanted to encourage people to tell their stories of diversity and so we asked a number of people to share their testimonies, some of which have already been quoted in this book. Here is another personal story, quoted in full:

Peter

I was born in Lambeth. My parents both came to England from
Jamaica in the early sixties. My father died when I was three,
leaving just my mother to bring up three boys (one of whom,
me, was deaf). During my childhood, I lived in council flats,
moving eight times in south London. My mother had a hard time
bringing us up. She had no extended family to support her. I
remember that food was scarce and often we went to bed hungry.

My childhood friendships were diverse: I often played with
the local children, both black and white, on the council estates.
In fact my best friend before I moved to the secondary deaf
school I attended, Oak Lodge, was an older, white hearing boy.
Together we got into a lot of mischief, such as setting off bangers
and posting them through letterboxes and daring each other to
carry out silly antics such as jumping from balconies. At that
time, I don't think I was aware of racial comments, as I obviously
couldn't hear them, and also I was just out looking for fun.

Communication at home with my mum was difficult. She didn't
'sign', and communication was through writing notes to each
other. Fortunately, my brothers could sign a little, which helped.

My mother suffered a nervous breakdown and we were put
into care while she recovered. I remember that, while at the
children's home, I was constantly attacked at night time when
I was sleeping. Children would hit me, make rude monkey
gestures, or during the day make fun of me because I was deaf.

However, my school experience was more positive. The
deaf school I attended was diverse. Children attended from
different cultures and this meant we accepted everyone. We had
a common bond – first and foremost we were deaf, and our skin
tone and culture were secondary.

Diversity has shaped my life. I have maintained the friendships
that I made at deaf school. Diversity has been with me my whole
life: I am a deaf, English, black man, and I married a hearing,

white, Scottish girl. We have three children, which society would label as 'mixed race', but for us they are children with a rich heritage which we want them to be proud of. Our aim for our children is to have a positive identity, to be proud of who they are and recognize that all people, regardless of race, colour and culture, are unique and special.

Fun – the celebration

At this level, freedom and fun are the main characteristics. You can laugh at your differences without the worry of causing offence or being offended. This is also the level at which a deep appreciation of the work of the cross – building bridges across hostile divides – comes to the fore, something you want to celebrate.

For the last few years at King's, we had an evening to celebrate our diversity. This evening came out of a desire to make more of Easter than we had done, and to link it with a celebration of diversity. We called the event 'Easter Now' and it became the second biggest event after Christmas. The reason we linked those two things together was the recognition that reconciliation across the divides was achieved at the cross. This was indeed Easter now! We worked hard on the programme to ensure that we faithfully retold the Easter story, celebrating and reflecting our diversity in the way we did it. We would include contributions from our children, from our deaf community and from different language groups. Over the years we had songs, poetry, PowerPoint presentations and drama. We encouraged people either to dress smartly or to come in cultural dress, and we had food which would reflect some of the many different nations represented at church. These evenings were open to guests from outside the church. Just observing the event was a powerful witness to diversity in unity achieved at the cross.

A relationship that epitomizes the two deepest levels described is my marriage to Pauline, a white British girl from Kent. We speak openly together about issues of race and diversity. This has brought us closer together and given both of us deeper levels of understanding and appreciation of our differences. It has also created a great deal of laughter and fun as we have highlighted aspects of our differences that we have found amusing.

Let me give you one such example that we now regularly laugh about. Not long after we were married, we heard a knock on the window of the bedroom of our ground floor flat. It was after 11 pm, we were in bed, and the flat was in darkness. As I remember it, Pauline stiffened, frightened, and I was the courageous husband who went to the door to find out who was there. It was my mum. She had come to find out how we were and had brought with her a banana cake! Pauline could never understand those late-night visits or phone calls. Her parents would never have called us after 9.30 pm if it hadn't been an emergency, or without prior notice.

I am also fortunate to have friends with whom we love to spend time laughing at our differences. When you are in a relationship where people really know and accept you, my experience is that there need be no fear of offence or being misunderstood. Obviously, reaching this level of relationship is not something that can happen overnight. It takes time and requires a building up of trust. But it is possible to get to a point of such freedom in a relationship that you don't constantly feel afraid that you may be treading on eggshells when you say something.

When I visited Bridgeway Community Church in Baltimore, Maryland, for their fifteenth anniversary, I was pleasantly surprised and encouraged by how much laughter and fun there was among the people there, as they celebrated their differences together as a church. So often, issues surrounding diversity can come across as heavy and challenging, but actually celebration, fun and laughter also have an important part to play.

Practical ways of reaching out

Here are some practical steps towards reaching across the divide in our relationships, whatever the divide in any type of friendship:

Prayer

It is not possible to develop relationships with everyone you meet, so ask God to make you open to the Holy Spirit's leading regarding which relationships to pursue and develop.

Time

Don't expect overnight change or complete understanding and effortless progress.

Mutual benefit

Relationships across the divide are not purely about mission or obedience. They are about developing personal friendships that benefit both groups and individuals.

Helping and being helped

Sometimes it is actually easier to help others than to receive help yourself. Be willing to be helped as you seek to reach across the divide. This may be in small ways, such as receiving food or practical support.

Be open and vulnerable

Whom do you go to when things hurt, or when you are making a major decision in your life? I know that I have a variety of good friends that I go to for input when I'm facing a new challenge. It is important to be open and vulnerable when crossing the divide.

Be genuine

Don't reach out to people across the divide purely for strategic reasons or to ease your conscience. Make your attempts genuine expressions of friendship. I once reached across a divide to someone who later indicated that they felt I had my own agenda in doing so. This was not true, but clearly this had been perceived in my actions. I apologized and have been much more aware of this pitfall ever since.

Show people they are valued

Express an interest in people's families and lives, and share information about your family and life too. You can do this by offering and receiving help, by giving and asking for advice, all of which shows the mutuality of the relationship.

Show interest in cultural issues and history

People are often very happy to talk about their culture and history. Ask questions. A word of caution, however: be wise as to how you do this, particularly if you are speaking to people whose nations have had a difficult or negative history.

Learn to relax

Be relaxed around people who are different. This takes time, but surely it must be one of our aims. We don't want every relationship across the divide to be a huge effort.

Don't give up

Don't take it personally if relationships across the divide begin slowly and even tentatively. Trust and acceptance take time to develop. My observation and experience is that many people are keen to develop relationships with people who are not like themselves, so don't give up easily.

To sum up ...

It might be that this book is beginning to give you not only a desire to reach across the divide, but permission to do so. I hope this chapter has helped you to identify some ways you might go about doing this. My prayer is that reading this book will help you to work out where you are, and ways in which you can move on to the next level. By engaging and changing, you are entering into the very purposes of God for his world, right now. As one of the chapter headings in Bruce Milne's *Dynamic Diversity* says, this is 'An idea whose hour has come: into the world of today'.

Questions for discussion

What prevents us from developing cross-cultural relationships?

What can we do to overcome these barriers?

How often have you shared communion, and celebrated reconciliation across the divides when doing so?

Are there other forms of diversity for which you need to cross the divide in your relationships?

8. HOW DO WE INTEGRATE PEOPLE FROM DIFFERENT BACKGROUNDS INTO CHURCH LIFE?

The fruit bowl

It's impossible not to find the idea of a fruit bowl with many different kinds of fruit appealing. A good fruit bowl will have apples, oranges, grapes, pears, bananas, kiwis, and maybe a pineapple in the middle for good measure. It can look fantastic. Most people like fruit and, best of all, it's good for you!

My three girls all love fruit. We always have a large bowl of fruit at home, which they regularly pick from. (They also like chocolate and sweets, just so that you don't get the wrong impression!) A fruit bowl made up of different fruits is the way it was meant to be. It looks great. However, up close we realize that oranges are not the same as apples, and pears are different from grapes. Kiwis are small and furry; bananas are an awkward shape. Oranges can be difficult to peel. You can eat the skins of apples, pears and grapes, but not oranges, bananas or mangos. They not only look different, but they also taste different. Most people prefer a mixed fruit bowl rather than just a bowl of apples.

And not all fruit is produced in the same way. Bananas and apples are grown in very different environments, and develop at different rates. Different types of fruit need to be treated differently. Soft fruits such as strawberries need much more careful handling than other fruits, like oranges.

In the same way, many people like the idea of diversity in the church. To be part of a diverse church, with people from different social backgrounds and different races and language groups, is actually quite appealing. When we see photos of church congregations, or attend church, we love the idea of different faces and races: young, old, black and white, and everything in between, all being together.

However, the reality of a multicultural church can be different. Some people have different skin colours, some appear awkward, some speak with different accents, and some speak completely different languages. Others take longer to get to know, and still others need more careful handling, being softer on the outside. Having all these different cultures in close proximity brings with it new and different challenges from those we may have faced before, particularly in the areas of language, worship, leadership and friendship. Yet the church was always meant to be made up of different cultures and peoples rubbing up against one another. A diverse church is not just supposed to look good in a photo of people worshipping together; it has a purpose far beyond that: to bring glory to God.

Now, if a church is made up of just one type of culture or race and wants to make room for other types, it may have to diversify its systems and methods of integration in order to encourage those coming in. It may have to start to do some things differently. Diversity is not simply about having people who are different join our churches, but also about embracing those differences. Ultimately, for diversity to work in the church, we all need to change.

Models of integration

This leads to a number of questions. How do we build diverse churches? How do we integrate people who are different from us? In what ways must we change to make room for them, and in what ways do those coming in need to change in order to join us? What will diversity look like in my church context? These are questions not only for churches, but for whole communities and countries as well.

I want to explore three models of social integration, and in each case look at how they work on a national scale and also in a local church context.

Assimilation model

Definition

Assimilation is the process of integration whereby immigrants, or other minority groups, are 'absorbed' into a generally larger community. This presumes a loss of all characteristics which make the newcomers different.

Strengths

- It retains a level of national unity and conformity
- It is better to assimilate than to segregate
- It is easy to manage

Weaknesses

- There is a loss of individual cultural identity (languages or traditions) of immigrants

- It is intolerant and requires that minority groups change
- It can lead to feelings of resentment among groups being assimilated

Other factors

- It can lead to tighter immigration controls
- It can have a strong nationalistic bias
- There is pressure on minorities to conform

Example from France

The French system does not distinguish between the ethnicity of its nationals. There aren't Algerian-French or Moroccan-French people, only French people. All are equal under French law. Tim King, writing in *Prospect* magazine, puts it this way: 'When an immigrant comes to France, he must drop everything he has learned of his previous culture; he has to leave it in his baggage.'

A study in 2004 showed two French citizens of similar age and with similar qualifications applying for jobs. One, with the classic French name François, obtained 75 out of 100 interviews, while the other, with the Algerian name Abdul, obtained 14 out of 100 interviews. Under the French system, this result would be merely a coincidence, because both men are French citizens with equal rights and status under the law.

What does an assimilated church look like?

In a church which assimilates people from minority groups, the majority group has to make room for those coming in, but most of the changing is done by the minority groups. In an assimilated church, diversity is managed rather than valued. Below is a list of characteristics and examples of an assimilating church.

Strengths

- There is a common focus
- It is easier to lead, as differences are less pronounced
- There is strong ownership by the majority group

Weaknesses

- Leadership roles are filled by one cultural group
- Teaching/worship styles do not necessarily take account of diversity
- Minority groups have to conform in order to integrate
- Minority groups can often remain on the edge of church life

Other factors

- *Representation is important*

  While I don't believe that churches are either democracies or even aiming for proportional representation, I do believe that any church growing in diversity ought to make room for leaders of diverse backgrounds to take on key roles and positions of influence. People who visit your church are asking, among other things, 'Is there room for me here?' They will answer this question in a number of ways, one of which will be by subconsciously observing who your leaders are. The expectation is not necessarily that their particular group is represented, but that there is a level of diversity in the leadership team.
- *Leadership development presents a challenge*

  When looking to develop other leaders, leaders often look for the obvious qualities that they themselves possess. Sometimes these qualities are more cultural than we realize, for leadership does not look the same in every culture. For example, in some cultures, taking initiative can be the mark of a leader. People who demonstrate good initiative may be seen as having potential leadership qualities. In other cultures, to take initiative may be seen as being too forward or pushy. Offering to take part without being asked or invited would be uncommon in some cultures.

My wife was once a juror in a criminal trial at a local crown court. She told me the story of how the jury picked its foreman. She asked her fellow jurors whether any of them had any management or leadership experience. One older gentleman indicated that he had, and he was duly elected as the foreman for the jury. My wife said that, as their discussions got under way, the 'real' leader of the group emerged: the one whose view carried most influence around the table and whose suggestions were most readily accepted. He was from a minority culture and had more relevant experience, yet he had not stepped forward when the opportunity had come up. It is not always easy to recognize leadership in different cultures, but being aware that some aspects of it might look different from your own culture will help.

• *The 'one-size-fits-all' mentality can be a blind spot*

Sometimes we think that everyone who joins the church will get involved in the same way. For example, in some churches there are restrictions on your level of involvement until you have been through the church membership process. In order to become a member, you may have to attend the eight-week membership course on a Tuesday evening. In the past, this may have worked for new people from a similar background as

the majority culture. But for your increasing number
of single parents, or people working longer hours and
more varied shift patterns, or immigrants from abroad,
this process may not always work. The result can be
that new people are less likely to become members
because they cannot do the course, which in turn
restricts their level of involvement. In other churches,
relationships with certain leaders are important in order
to gain the trust required to serve in the church.

- *Some people want to belong before they believe*
  Another shift is taking place in some churches:
  people are happy to belong before they believe. Before
  they come to faith and take on your values, they want
  to be part of your community and serve. Taking the
  radical step of finding ways of allowing people who are
  unchurched to be part of your community is exciting,
  but also challenging, for an assimilating church.
  Obviously, key roles, such as any leadership role, must
  remain in the remit of members. You may need to
  decide where you stand regarding seekers who want to
  serve before they have come right through to faith.

Pluralistic model
Definition
Pluralism is a system that includes individuals from groups
with different basic background experiences and cultures.
Pluralism primarily preserves the right of each group to
maintain its cultural heritage. It implies mutual respect.

Strengths

- Cultural distinctives are retained
- It is more tolerant of diversity
- It recognizes and values difference

Weaknesses

- It allows ethnic divisions (segregation)
- The majority culture can feel displaced by the emphasis on diversity
- People can fear the erosion of national identity, history, tradition and culture

Other factors

- It allows more immigration
- Positive discrimination can occur
- Cross-cultural awareness is encouraged

Example from the UK

The UK is a pluralistic nation. Our form of integration is called 'multiculturalism'. During the 1980s and 1990s, multiculturalism became the dominant approach in conducting Britain's race relations. Racial equality was understood not as enabling ethnic minorities to become more like the dominant majority, but as the equal right of each ethnic group to assert its own identity. This has resulted in people being born and brought up in the UK with no allegiance to the nation in which they live. Multiculturalism also erodes Christian values in order to embrace and value other religions and faiths.

Multiculturalism is being challenged and potentially redefined as a means of integration. There are a number of reasons for this, a key one being that it has not created a common identity for all people to connect with, and can therefore appear divisive.

What does a pluralistic church look like?

A pluralistic approach to church life involves making room for others coming in, but not necessarily requiring them to change. New groups are valued and allowed to express themselves alongside the majority culture.

Strengths

- It allows for diversity in leadership
- It encourages a diverse congregation
- It celebrates diversity

Weaknesses

- It can celebrate diversity with little acknowledgement of the majority culture
- Different cultural groups are not necessarily encouraged to mix
- There are separate meetings for different groups
- There is no clear overall identity but lots of individual group identities

Other factors

- *Language is an important issue*
  Where there are different languages, separate meetings can sometimes be helpful. In my view, however, these should not occur any more often than when the church comes together as a corporate body. Where possible and practical, if sufficient non-English speakers are present, all using the same language, interpretation should be offered. There is something even more important than the desire to meet individual

cultural needs: namely, being together as one people
and building relationships across the divide.

- *Churches play a key role*

   Churches can also play a key role in helping speakers
of other languages to learn English. This helps in
building relationships, and also in the integration
of people into society at large. Churches should
encourage people not merely to learn other languages,
but also to teach English to speakers of other languages.
My experience of those who come from abroad to the
UK is that they want to learn English. As mentioned
in a previous chapter, one of the members of King's
Church runs a school teaching English for Speakers of
Other Languages (ESOL). Out of that school, a number
of people have begun to attend church, become
Christians, and then been baptized.

- *Deaf people*

   Churches should encourage relationships between
hearing and deaf people, wherever possible. As a local
church, King's Church provides British Sign Language
(BSL) interpretation every week at one of the services.
There are also small groups for deaf people, and for deaf
and hearing people together. Once a month, the deaf
community will have their own meeting, with worship
and a talk by some of the deaf leaders, or by a hearing
person who signs well or is supported by an interpreter.
Some deaf people prefer to remain in the main meeting
with interpretation, while others come only when there
is a deaf service.

   Our aim is integration wherever possible, but we
must also recognize and acknowledge the particular
needs of a group which is able to integrate only in
certain ways.

Integrated model
Definition

Integration is a system that encourages you to keep your cultural distinctives while adopting a common identity. You consider yourself a citizen of your new nation first, and the nation of your birth second.

Strengths

- Allows for common identity and therefore unity
- Allows, at the same time, for cultural differences to be expressed

Weaknesses

- This is a very difficult balance to achieve
- It still requires that those coming in are persuaded to lose something of their cultural identity, but hopefully for a greater gain
- It also requires that the host nation residents potentially lose something of their heritage

Other factors

- It requires greater levels of cross-cultural relationships than the other models

Example from the USA

There is no perfect example of this model, but in the USA everyone has a level of patriotism while holding on to some traditional or cultural heritage. Even Martin Luther King did not fight purely for equality and his civil rights. He saw this very much as part of the 'American dream'.

What does an integrated church look like?

A truly integrated church will not only manage and value diversity, but embrace it as well. Both the majority and minority groups will need to change in order to embrace diversity.

Strengths

- A strong common identity – in Christ and in the local church
- A diverse leadership team in which all leaders embrace and make room for diversity: for example, leaders show awareness of diversity in their preaching illustrations
- People from diverse backgrounds are encouraged to pursue meaningful relationships across the divide

Weaknesses

- There are not many good examples to follow
- The majority culture may be unwilling not just to make room, but to change
- It is dependent on the strength of the leader's internal conviction that this is the right way
- There is more potential for conflict due to misunderstandings

Other factors

- *The Antioch church model*

  The Antioch congregation lived out an inclusive table fellowship that emulated the social practices of Jesus. Each person who joined the fellowship felt affirmed for the culture of his or her background. Yet each also adopted a higher calling through allegiance to Jesus Christ. Jews and Gentiles continued to embrace their culture of origin but broke with certain cultural rules that inhibited their ability to live as one in Christ. For example they ate and socialised together. While this was not permitted or approved of in society, in 'the many house-congregations' of Antioch ... Jews and Gentiles, living together in crowded city quarters, freely mixed.

In Antioch we have an example of a truly integrated church where people felt affirmed in their own culture, but adopted the higher calling of the Christian. Following Christ came first, and at times this meant sacrificing something of their culture.

The challenge is in recognizing which of our treasured values and practices are cultural expressions, and which are truly Christian expressions of faith.

A diversity of approach

The overall aim is for integration and diversity in church, as much as possible. However, in some situations it would seem to me beneficial to either assimilate or work alongside other cultures or groups. I have already given language as an ideal example of assimilating, but recognizing a pluralistic approach may be the best way initially. Another area of church life where a pluralistic approach might be helpful is in outreach or evangelism. Sometimes it is better to show understanding and appreciation of where someone is coming from, as part of your desire to reach them, than just expecting them either to integrate or be assimilated into your ways.

On our Alpha course, which provides people who want to explore Christianity an opportunity to do so, we have different groups, depending on where people are coming from: groups for young people, or various language groups, all operating separately. It may be that we need to take a variety of approaches towards different aspects of church life.

Growth, diversity and the organizational challenge

One of the potential weaknesses of an integrated church, which I have alluded to already, is conflict because of misunderstandings. A general challenge to diverse churches will be conflict from cross-cultural issues or, at the very least, *perceived* issues. Even perceived issues are real to the person with the perception. It is better to take the approach that something is an issue rather than argue about whether or not it is real. Finding a way to handle the issue is important if true diversity in unity is going to be achieved, and relationships across the divide are going to be developed.

Growth and diversity lead to organizational challenges. Handled well, they can lead to further growth, greater unity, and ever-increasing mission opportunities. Handled poorly, they can hold back growth and create disunity. Let me explain with reference to a passage of Scripture that shows the importance of organization.

> In those days when the number of disciples was increasing, the Grecian Jews among them complained against the Hebraic Jews because their widows were being overlooked in the daily distribution of food. So the Twelve gathered all the disciples together and said, 'It would not be right for us to neglect the ministry of the word of God in order to wait on tables. Brothers, choose seven men from among you who are known to be full of the Spirit and wisdom. We will turn this responsibility over to them and will give our attention to prayer and the ministry of the word.'
>
> This proposal pleased the whole group. They chose Stephen, a man full of faith and of the Holy Spirit; also Philip, Procorus,

Nicanor, Timon, Parmenas, and Nicolas from Antioch, a convert
to Judaism. They presented these men to the apostles, who
prayed and laid their hands on them.

So the word of God spread. The number of disciples in
Jerusalem increased rapidly, and a large number of priests became
obedient to the faith.

(Acts 6:1–7)

The church had seen remarkable growth. Not only were
people being saved and added, but their needs were also
being met. Acts 4:34 states, 'There were no needy persons
among them.' They had a reputation for generosity, and
the apostles had an important role in organizing the gener-
ous donations to meet the needs of the people. By Acts 6,
this strength had become a potential weakness, because
of growth which included some elements of diversity. A
problem which could have caused disunity had arisen.

What was the main problem?

In summary, the problem was discrimination. This was both
cultural and religious, and possibly included language issues.
All the people involved were of Jewish origin, but from different backgrounds. There is a very good chance that the
discrimination was unwitting rather than deliberate, but it
was discrimination all the same.

For whatever reason, the Greek-speaking Jewish widows
(a minority group, probably from the Jewish Diaspora) had
been overlooked when it came to the distribution of food
in the church. They were missing out. The complaint came
to the apostles, who set an excellent example of dealing
with the discrimination of minority or vulnerable people.
They also show us the importance of organization and the
implementation of vision.

What did the apostles do?

- *They listened*

    This may appear obvious, but it is fundamental. They were willing to hear the complaint and act on it. Such an approach gives value to those who feel discriminated against and those who speak up for them.

- *They focused on the complaint, not the complainant*

    The Greeks stood up for their widows. They spotted the problem first and made a complaint to the Hebraic Jews. Sometimes people need to stand up for their people. Mother Teresa became the voice of the poor in Calcutta and stood before presidents and kings as an advocate for the poor. Both Gandhi and Nelson Mandela are also examples of people who stood up for their people. Closer to home, Joel Edwards, the former General Director of the Evangelical Alliance, stood up and represented over a million Christians in the UK, in an increasingly secular society. The apostles did not allow themselves to be distracted by focusing on the complainants, but rather focused on the complaint.

- *They took the complaint seriously*

    The apostles made no excuses or denials (Acts 6:2–4). It would have been very easy to get defensive; even to try to cover it up. Denial of a complaint can do as much damage as the incident that led to the complaint in the first place. The apostles took the complaint seriously and acted quickly, all of which would have gone some way to ensuring that the church stayed united after the complaint had been dealt with.

- *They brought the complaint to all the disciples*

    The apostles were aware of their need for help in handling the task (verse 2) and they also recognized that the problem itself could affect everyone. It was not just a problem for the Greek widows.

- *They clarified their roles and responsibilities*

The apostles were able to clarify that they felt their primary call and ministry was the word and prayer (2, 4). Up to this point, the apostles had also been responsible for the distribution of food to the widows. Growth was making it difficult for them to meet all their responsibilities. By clarifying their responsibilities, they dealt with people's expectations. They didn't reduce the importance of what needed to be done, but rather made sure those responsibilities were better administered.

- *They allowed the disciples to be involved in finding a solution*

We see the apostles involving the disciples (3), and as a result the apostles gained ownership and expert help, while they themselves remained free to focus on their primary responsibilities.

- *They saw the organization of such a task as an important spiritual function*

Administration was not considered an unimportant practical task, but a key spiritual function (3). As a result, there was a need for criteria for those who would carry out this responsibility. You cannot overestimate the role of administration and organization in ensuring that the church fulfils its mission. Furthermore, administration can either help or hinder unity in the church.

- *They chose men who were full of the Spirit and wisdom*

The apostles gained ownership from the people who made the complaint by choosing men with good reputations and wisdom, full of the Holy Spirit (5). This would have required recognizing leadership qualities in people from different backgrounds.

What was the result?

As a result of the apostles' actions, growth in the church continued (7).

This was not a small sideline issue: the growth and unity of the church had been at stake here. Wrongly handled, growth might have slowed down or stopped, and quite possibly the church could have split. Here, growth appears to be a sign that the apostles got it right, and so God's blessing continued in the Jerusalem church. Interestingly, this growth involved a large number of priests becoming obedient to the faith. Could it be that people had been watching to see how the church would deal with a problem that was not uncommon: tension between people groups and issues of discrimination? Is the obedience of the priests a sign that if the church handles issues of diversity well, it can lead to real mission progress among those of the establishment and recognized institutions also grappling with these issues?

How do we apply these truths today?

When somebody sees a problem and makes a complaint, it can be easy to make them the issue rather than to focus on the issue itself.

All complaints should be taken seriously. It is true that some may be spurious, but it is better initially to take all complaints seriously and thereby ensure that genuine complaints are properly dealt with.

Make sure that administrative systems and processes do not account only for growth, but also for the diversity of growth. For example, as a result of a growth in diversity, you may start a group teaching English for Speakers of Other Languages, or some people might learn British Sign Language. Others may even become familiar with local issues of immigration in order to help others. I remember attending one church which was saying goodbye to two teenage refugee girls who had found their way into a foreign country, city and local church. Their story was a heart-rending one of pain, anguish and displacement. The church had not only put them up, but had acted as their advocates with the immigration authorities. The girls were now going to live with relatives in another country.

Administrators need to have a vision for diversity and to understand that this is part of their role and responsibility. So often, administrators are the 'front door' of your church and the first contact someone with a problem will talk to. They are crucial implementers of the church's vision for diversity in unity.

To sum up ...

When churches make room for others, and change in order to embrace others, administrators must also be involved. Otherwise, people may hear that the church values diversity and wants to embrace it, but their experience is anything but embracing!

In this chapter I have looked at how we integrate people from different backgrounds into church life. The underlying keys to this are: recognizing that systems and processes may have to change to embrace diversity; recognizing that *we* may have to change to embrace diversity; and the importance of organization as churches grow in diversity.

Questions for discussion

Think about which approach best describes the church you are part of.

What are the strengths and weaknesses in the ways new people join your church?

How well do you listen to other people?

In what ways can organization help diversity?

9. WHAT DOES A TRULY DIVERSE CHURCH LOOK LIKE?

A truly diverse congregation where anybody enjoys more than 75% of what's going on is not thoroughly integrated . . . So an integrating church is characterized by the need to be content with less than total satisfaction of anything. You have to factor in a willingness to absorb some things that are not dear to you but may be precious to some of those coming in.

These are the words of Dr James Forbes, Senior Minister Emeritus of The Riverside Church in New York, a multi-cultural church made up of over 2,000 people. Forbes' statement gets right to the heart of the issue: in order to make room for diversity as new people come in, things will have to change. Some of us are quite willing to change, but we just don't know what to change and what it will look like. Jesus gives us a good example of the need for humility and a servant heart (Matthew 20:25–28), which should characterize our response to change. Our desire should be to see others blessed and their needs met, rather than thinking only of ourselves.

You will know from my introduction that I have sought to answer some of the questions that I have heard asked, and have asked myself, about diversity in the church. Growing diversity causes us to ask questions that we didn't even know were there before. There are two areas we have not yet covered, and it is important that we cover them now if we wish to be able truly to move on. First, what does a truly diverse church look like? Secondly, where do I start and what is the next step for me and the church I attend? In this chapter I want to look at these questions: What does a church growing in diversity really look like? How can we tell we are on the right track? What are the shared characteristics of such churches and what are their distinctives?

First, I should say right up front that there aren't too many examples of truly diverse churches, that have both grown in diversity in their congregations and actively begun to work through some of the issues. It is certainly not my aim to try to limit what God can do, and is doing, through his church, so this chapter will contain some unashamedly idealistic and visionary ideas, as well as some measurable and more real-istic aims. Before exploring some of the more fundamental aspects of truly diverse churches, let me make a few more general comments.

Advice for a church seeking to be diverse

All will look different

In many ways, there can be no 'one-size-fits-all' approach to churches that are truly diverse. By definition, there is some difference in how these churches will operate and look. There will be differences in how pastoral care operates, how small groups work, how the leadership team functions, and how worship is expressed. In that sense, there can be no blueprint. Also, the diversities are not necessarily going to be the same. No two churches will be made up of the same different groups of people. As Bruce Milne states in *Dynamic Diversity*, 'How the principles of the new-humanity church are worked out in each local setting will patently be a matter of very considerable diversity.'

Change takes time

The truth is that churches are always changing – they are not supposed to be static. Change is either that of life, progress and growth or, unfortunately, that of decline. It is certainly the case that some churches are moving towards being truly diverse, but are not there yet. They are working hard to bring diversity into key aspects of church life, but there are still a number of elements not yet in place. Change rarely happens overnight, particularly if a church has only begun to experience diversity relatively recently, or is reacting to the diversity it is experiencing. Part of the skill here for leaders is the management of change and diversity. Steve Tibbert, Senior Pastor at King's Church, has said on many occasions, 'Diversity is complex and impacts every level of church life.'

It's all about the local church

I am convinced that what we have been talking about in this book will be best worked out in truly diverse local church congregations, not merely in situations where different churches with black or white majorities come together to share fellowship across the divide, although this may be a good place to start. Every local church, regardless of where it is, ought to be seeking to reach out to the whole community around it, not only to a part. For example, a black-majority church in London should be reaching out to all people in its vicinity, not just to black people. It is in the context of the local church and personal relationships that many of our New Testament examples of cross-cultural encounters come: Jesus' relationship with his disciples and their relationships with one another were affected by their different backgrounds. The apostle Paul and the apostle Peter grappled with diversity issues in local church contexts: in Galatia, Ephesus, Antioch and Macedonia. Also, God makes his promise plain in Scripture: 'His intent was that now, *through the church* [my emphasis], the manifold wisdom of God should be made known ... according to his eternal purpose which he accomplished in Christ ... ' (Ephesians 3:10–11). For diversity to get personal, it must get local, and be worked out in local church congregations and communities.

Avoid the politics of diversity

Diversity in our nation has a strong political aspect. While there is some value in that, this is not necessarily the model the church ought to be following. Our blueprint for diversity ought to come from what the Bible says and not from how our culture handles it. Jesus encouraged his disciples to take a different approach: 'You know that the rulers of the Gentiles lord it over them, and their high officials exercise authority over them. Not so with you' (Matthew 20:25–26). The Bible actually has a lot to say about our relationships across the divide. We, the church, have been given the Holy Spirit and the Word of God to help and guide us in fulfilling God's purpose on the earth. It is not equality that the Bible advocates, but rather justice and radical inclusiveness. Our churches should be advocates of the same.

The 80/20 principle

George Yancey, in his helpful book *One Body, One Spirit*, says, 'A multiracial church is a church in which no one racial group makes up more than 80% of the attendees of at least one of the major worship services.' This can only be seen as a guide, as some churches can have a very diverse and inclusive feel even though they don't meet this standard.

Four distinctives of a truly diverse church

I now want to focus on four fundamental distinctives which every multicultural church should have, or at least be actively working towards, in order to be considered truly diverse. The purpose of this is to help churches assess where they are on the journey and where they are heading.

Theology of diversity

Every church needs to have a growing understanding of the theology of diversity, in the same way that it has an understanding of the person and work of the Holy Spirit.

> I will make you into a great nation
>> and I will bless you;
> I will make your name great,
>> and you will be a blessing.
> I will bless those who bless you,
>> and whoever curses you I will curse;
> and all peoples on earth
>> will be blessed through you.
>
> (Genesis 12:2–3)

God's plan for diverse community was in his heart from the beginning. Throughout the Old Testament, he reminds his people that he does not look only *to* them, but also *beyond* them.

> In that day there will be a highway from Egypt to Assyria. The Assyrians will go to Egypt and the Egyptians to Assyria. The Egyptians and Assyrians will worship together. In that day Israel will be the third, along with Egypt and Assyria, a blessing on the earth. The LORD Almighty will bless them, saying, 'Blessed be Egypt my people, Assyria my handiwork, and Israel my inheritance.' (Isaiah 19:23–25)

The Egyptians and Assyrians represented two of the evil oppressors of the people of Israel in the Old Testament. Unlikely people and groups were to be included with the people of God, in order that God would demonstrate something of who he is and the fact that he is Lord over all.

Then, in the New Testament, we see the ultimate fulfilment of his great plan at the cross, where Jesus removed the barriers of sin that separated us from God and those that separated us from one another. Pentecost represents a moment in history when God's blessing was poured out on people from 'every nation under heaven' (Acts 2:5). Here is a reversal of the judgment that brought separation at the Tower of Babel.

The story reaches a crescendo in the book of Revelation when we catch a glimpse of the church at the end of time. 'I saw the Holy City, the new Jerusalem, coming down out of heaven from God, prepared as a bride beautifully dressed for her husband' (Revelation 21:2). God is preparing a bride for his Son. The church, made up of the people of God, is that bride coming together in all her diversity and unity, a fitting partner for the Son. The key here is not that we don't believe it, but that we are to be pursuing that diversity in unity while we are here on earth.

Diversity in leadership

'In the church at Antioch there were prophets and teachers: Barnabas, Simeon called Niger, Lucius of Cyrene, Manaen (who had been brought up with Herod the Tetrarch) and Saul' (Acts 13:1).

The Antioch church had a number of leaders from different backgrounds. What we notice is that this team were *together* as they prayed and fasted and sought God. They were together in their decision to set apart Paul and Barnabas for the work. For them to set apart Paul and Barnabas communicates that they had real power and authority to lead.

Other cultures

Achieving recognition of leaders from other cultures can be one of the hardest things, but it is vital if the church is to be taken seriously and seen as genuinely diverse. If a truly diverse church is what we are aiming for, we need to learn to trust God not simply to bring people, but also leaders from other cultures.

Different generations

The apostle Paul told Timothy not to allow anyone to look down on him because he was young (1 Timothy 4:12). Leadership has two opposite dangers when it comes to age. First, leaders and leadership teams can grow old quickly and sometimes forget how young they were when they started out, and so they expect the next generation to reach a certain maturity before bringing them through. Secondly, we can sometimes focus so much on raising younger leaders that we forget that older leaders have an important part to play. In and of itself, age should be no barrier to leadership, any more than race or cultural background.

Real responsibility and authority

Leadership must not be a form of tokenism: a position without power, influence and authority. Leaders should be given real authority in the roles and responsibilities they have. From my own experience as a leader, I know the importance of this. Part of my confidence came from knowing I was trusted and had the backing of other elders, in particular the lead elder, Steve Tibbert. In the early days of leadership, this was very important to me as I was the only black leader in a predominately white church. Some people had never been led or managed by a black person before, and so I needed to win their trust. Partly, this was achieved through the trust and authority obviously invested in me by Steve and the other leaders.

Representing the church, not just a minority group

Leaders from minority groups are not brought into position just to represent a minority group. Leaders should be appointed as a result of a recognition of gifting, anointing and confirmation of a good character which is observed by all. There may be leaders who emerge within particular groups, but the aim is to have a diverse leadership team whose members lead across the church, as in Antioch, not just a minority group. A good example of this was in South Lee Church in south east London, where there were three elders, one of whom, Paul Floyd, was deaf. Paul, who passed away in 2008, wasn't an elder for deaf people, but one of the elders over the whole church. He was also a great advocate for reaching across the divide between deaf and hearing people in churches.

Diversity in worship

'My house will be called a house of prayer for all nations'
(Mark 11:17).

Inclusive service

When the church comes together, an expression of who we
are in terms of diversity should be a regular feature of our
meetings, whether through the worship time, sermon or at
some other point during the service. Jesus' prophetic word
was that his house would be for all people, an inclusive place
where people from all backgrounds could come, pray and
worship God together. Worship in that sense must be inclusive and allow for all parts of the community to be engaged.
Breaking bread as part of worship takes on a new significance
when our reflection focuses not only on how Jesus' sacrifice
sets us free to come into a relationship with God, but also on
how it unites us with brothers and sisters who look, sound
and act differently from us. The cross goes even further,
according to the apostle Paul's letter to the Ephesians: his
death makes family members out of strangers, and friends out
of enemies (Ephesians 2:11–22). I experience this dynamic for
myself every time we break bread in church.

Another example of being inclusive in worship is in the
area of corporate prayer. This can relate both to the content
of the prayers, thanking God for our diversity in unity won
at the cross, or praying for different nations around the
world represented in our church, but also in the language
in which prayers are prayed. We can express our diversity
by making space for people to pray in their own language,
where this is appropriate.

Style

Diversity in style doesn't necessarily mean that, in a single worship service, you try to please everyone by starting with a hymn, followed by a contemporary guitar-based worship song, leading into some Christian hip-hop, and finishing with a good old gospel number sung in Spanish! We must never forget that worship is ultimately for God, not for us. Introducing different styles of worship probably takes longer than people think, as it requires musicians who can play in styles with which they are not necessarily familiar. A danger is that worship can become 'need-driven', in that we can become too particular about what songs we sing and in which style we play them. While you may want to look at different genres of songs, keep looking out for those that are full of biblical truth, have inclusive language, and are positive expressions of diversity. 'In Christ alone my hope is found' is an example of a song with an inclusive phrase that every Christian can relate to, regardless of background and culture.

Team personnel

In some ways, it can prove easier to include people from different backgrounds in worship than actually to change the style of worship. The important element here is continually to make it known that you are open to, and indeed desire, people from other backgrounds to be part of the worship team. Those who oversee and lead worship need to find ways and systems to help recruit people from diverse backgrounds who use musical styles different from their own. Not every budding singer from a minority group in your church will volunteer to sing. Choirs are growing in popularity, not only in the church, but as a local community social activity. In churches, they are a great way to reflect your diversity, and an easy first step for the person who wants to sing.

Diversity in relationships

'This mystery is that through the gospel the Gentiles are heirs together with Israel, members together of one body, and sharers together in the promise in Christ Jesus' (Ephesians 3:6).

One of the mysteries of the church is that people are brought together. This is another fundamental key to a truly diverse church: it's about people coming together. A truly diverse church will have people meeting all together more often than they do in separate groups. I encouraged a church with a Spanish-speaking segment of the congregation to have more services together with the rest of the church than they did apart. This has practical implications in terms of needing to provide an interpreter, but it expresses a higher value of being together. Being together is a fundamental part of what Jesus achieved on the cross and part of God's ultimate purpose, and out of it relationships can develop. 'His purpose was to create in himself one new man out of the two, thus making peace, and in this one body to reconcile both of them to God through the cross, by which he put to death their hostility' (Ephesians 2:15–16).

According to John Piper, Senior Pastor of Bethlehem Baptist Church in Minneapolis, USA, 'Reconciliation across the divides has always been a blood of Christ issue.' This may be missed by most commentators and much of the church, but there in the pages of Scripture are similar battles to the ones we face around us: withdrawing from other groups, stereotyping people, and a negative history. In the pages of Scripture are God's promises of forgiveness and reconciliation.

The challenge for us is not only to believe, but to act. It takes more than the heart and the mouth to build a truly diverse church. It is not enough to want or intend to do something. God also calls us to act. I did not become a father simply by desiring to have children; rather, I did something about it! Reading books on being a good dad became helpful only when I became one. In the same way, one of the biggest challenges for us is not only persuading people that God calls us to build diverse churches that are radically inclusive, but rather actively working together to build them. This involves taking steps of faith and risks, as we move out of our comfort zone to put into practice what many of us already believe.

As you look at these four fundamental aspects of what it means to be truly diverse, aim to make progress in these areas.

How diverse is your church?

One of the ways in which we can measure progress in terms of our growth as a diverse church is through an annual, or biannual, review of where we are with the integration of diverse groups at all levels of church life. Using the four fundamental areas outlined above, I have devised a census below which churches can use to assess how much progress they are making year on year, and where they need to improve. In larger churches you could carry out a census for each area of ministry.

Strengths of a census

- It provides you with a snapshot of where you are on the journey
- It can identify areas for specific focus
- It can identify areas that are working well
- It can help you to become more intentional

Weaknesses of a census

- Statistics don't tell the whole story
- It can lead to you simply chasing percentage increases
- It can cause you to become complacent
- It does not account for the cultural feel or expression of the church

Leadership

What percentage of your regular congregation comes from minority groups?

What percentage of your wider leadership group comes from minority groups?

What percentage of your senior leaders/elders comes from minority groups?

How does this compare with the previous year's figures?

Can you give reasons for the progress you have/have not made?

Worship

What percentage of your worship leaders comes from minority groups?

What percentage of your singers/band comes from minority groups?

What percentage of other Sunday upfront ministries comes from minority groups?

How does this compare with the previous year's figures?

Can you give reasons for the progress you have/have not made?

Relationships

What percentage of your small groups comes from minority groups?

What percentage of your regular volunteers comes from minority groups?

What percentage of your membership list comes from minority groups?

What percentage of the new people you have met and shown hospitality to this year are from minority groups?

How does this compare with the previous year's figures?

Can you give reasons for the progress you have/have not made?

Theology

What have you done in the last year to increase your learning and understanding of a theology of diversity? Has diversity been taught or referred to in the church over the last twelve months?

Real examples

I would love to give lots of examples of churches that have made the journey, come out on the other side, and now stand as examples for all of us to follow, but the truth is that I can't. King's Church, Catford, my previous home church, is among a growing number of churches I know which are intentionally working through the issue of diversity. Like others, it has a long way to go. The truth is that no church will get all of these issues completely sorted out this side of heaven. This is not meant as some sort of 'cop out' statement, but reality. Embracing diversity in church does not mean perfection, but hopefully it does mean making progress towards being all that God desires and purposes his people to be. As we've seen, many churches around the UK are embracing diversity. Encouragingly, an increasing number of new churches are being planted in and around the cities all across this nation and are expressing a desire to build diverse communities of believers.

The best examples we have of truly diverse churches, together with the key principles for building them, are found in the Bible. The churches in Corinth, Ephesus, Rome, Colossae and Galatia grappled with this issue. We are now called to do the same and to follow the examples they have set. We do not do this alone, though. God comes in the form of the Holy Spirit to be our helper and our guide. The cross expresses to us the level of his commitment to this, and the emphatic nature of his victory over the segregation, division and separation sin has caused. His word tells us that he has chosen, in his wisdom and grace, to use us, his people the church, to display his glory, not just to the world, but to 'rulers and authorities in the heavenly realms' (Ephesians 3:10). Diversity began and will finish in him.

Questions for discussion

Do you agree with Dr James Forbes' statement quoted at the beginning of this chapter? Explain your reasons.

How diverse is the church you attend, bearing in mind the four fundamentals of diversity?

What action can you take as an individual to help your church truly to embrace diversity?

Try visiting a church that is more diverse than your own. What can you learn from the experience?

10. 'I WANT TO CROSS THE RACE DIVIDE, SO WHERE DO I START?'

Passive to active

As I mentioned earlier, towards the end of 2004 I took a trip to Cape Town, South Africa. On the last night, I and one of the other guys watched the stirring film *Cry Freedom*, which tells the story of the relationship between Steve Biko, a black political activist, and Donald Woods. Woods was the white editor of a South African national newspaper, *The Daily Dispatch*, based in East London, and a supporter of the anti-apartheid movement. The film tells the story of the meeting of these two men, the friendship that developed between them and their families, Biko's death, and the subsequent flight from South Africa of Woods and his family. I had seen the film before, but watching it in Cape Town, South Africa was quite poignant for me. The film begins in Crossroads, a township on the outskirts of Cape Town. Part of the film dramatized the sequence of events leading up to the murder of Steve Biko, which followed one of his visits to Cape Town and his subsequent arrest. A few days earlier, we had visited the townships that now stand on the Crossroads site. On this occasion, however, as I re-watched the film so close to the very neighbourhoods where some of the events had taken place, what struck me most were not so much the actions of Steve Biko, but rather those of Donald Woods.

At the very beginning, the film portrays Woods as what we might call a 'passive' supporter of the anti-apartheid movement. The film shows how Donald Woods shifted over time to become an activist. Fuelled by his relationship with Steve Biko, he gained understanding of black history and culture. He realized that it was not enough for him to be a passive supporter of a movement for change, but that he had to become active. As an activist, he was no longer fighting *their* cause; now it had become *his* cause. Eventually he was forced to leave South Africa with his family, because of threats to his life from the South African authorities. Following his departure, he and his family were granted political asylum in the UK. As a 'passive' supporter he had made some small changes consistent with his beliefs. He had employed both black and white journalists and had them seated together in his offices. He had been openly critical of government policy on certain occasions in his editorials, as he had been of some anti-apartheid groups. For a white editor of a South African national newspaper, these were radical moves. As he moved into the role of an activist, though, Woods brought the plight of Steve Biko to the world and deliberately began to use the public arena to shed further light on the horrors of apartheid. Donald Woods became the first private citizen to be given an invitation to address the UN Security Council. The book he subsequently wrote catapulted him and the anti-apartheid cause onto the international stage. He travelled all over the world, speaking against the apartheid system.

The film also portrays his wife as someone who came on board with his beliefs a little after him, but by doing so re-enforced them. She was what we might call a 're-activist' (see discussion on page 165). She also held similar beliefs to her husband and, as he changed, so did she. His cause became their cause. Her support strengthened and encouraged Woods to take the radical steps he did towards change.

Donald Woods was a passive anti-apartheid supporter who became an activist. In many ways, his basic beliefs did not change. He still believed apartheid was wrong, just as he always had done. When he became an activist, however, his attitude and actions changed, and this contributed to real and lasting change in the nation. As I watched that film once again, I realized that there were parallels in the way you and I may view and respond to diversity.

Below I have outlined the three positions: passive supporter, activist supporter and re-activist supporter. Let's take a look at each, and see if you can identify which one you feel best describes your current situation with regard to diversity.

Passive supporter

This is someone who is supportive of diversity but doesn't necessarily act on it in an intentional way.

As you've read this book, you have not needed much convincing of the importance of some of the issues raised. Like Donald Woods at the start of his journey, you are a passive supporter of diversity in the church. Fundamentally, you believe that God has called his people to be together and to display something of his glory to the world around us. Like Woods, you have made some changes, where these have been possible. Such changes might be as small as emotionally 'making room', as people who are different from you start coming to your church. Even reading this book has been a big step for you, and it has begun to fuel your desire to grow in awareness and reach out. I commend you for getting this far. I know this has probably not always been an easy book to read! Some of you passive supporters also desire to move on to become more active in embracing diversity. Maybe you have been inspired, as Donald Woods was, to take further steps. Let me suggest three things you can do:

- **Pray:** Ask God to open your eyes to see difference and open your heart to embrace it. As you seek to embrace diversity, be willing to deal with any attitudes that surface in your heart and mind. Reread the earlier chapter on forgiveness, if this helps.
- **Read** the Bible and become familiar with God's great plan 'to bring all things together ...'
- **Reach out:** Without trying to change the world overnight, reach out to people who may be different from you, whether it's someone who attends your church, a neighbour or a work colleague. If you have a family, reach out to another family from a different background. Be brave and take the initiative.

Activist supporter

This is someone who does not just hold a particular belief or view, but is active in seeking change and bringing light to others where change is needed.

You are among the frontline troops, the people who win battles, take ground and initiate change. There is no limit to what an activist can do once he or she has a worthy cause and a courageous heart. As an activist, you are prepared to

take steps to change things. You have gained some awareness and understanding of people who are different from
you, perhaps through showing hospitality or just pursuing
friendship. As a result, you are learning to appreciate difference. You have also realized that, in order to make real
progress in this area, you will need to become more active
and intentional. Diversity is no longer someone else's issue;
it has become your issue. Many activists are keen to move, so
here are some things you can do now:

- **Pray:** Ask God for an opportunity to initiate a
  conversation across the divide with a friend or key
  leaders. Do this with a hope of securing support
  for change.
- **Read** some good Christian books that tackle diversity
  (I have recommended some at the end).
- **Reach out:** Make connections and begin to develop
  relationships with people in your world who may be
  different from you, just like the passive supporter. Make
  sure that you also reach out to passive supporters and
  re-activists and help them to make progress.

Wherever you are, use your influence to reach out across
the divide. As you have read this book, you may have gained
ideas that can help you make further changes and progress.
If you hold a leadership position, then you can bring about
real change in whatever sphere you lead. Remember, a key
part of leadership is ensuring that the people you lead come
on the journey with you when you seek to make changes.
Press on and don't give up. At times, you may feel like you
are fighting against the world, but let me remind you what
the Bible says: 'the one who is in you is greater than the one
who is in the world' (1 John 4:4).

Re-activist supporter

This is my own term for someone who supports and encourages change, and helps to retain progress made.

Donald Woods' wife Wendy was a 're-activist'. Where he had clearly made this his cause, she supported and followed. She believed what he believed and took the family with her. Without her, Woods probably wouldn't have been anywhere near as effective as he was. Re-activists are early adopters of change, or at the very least key adopters. Perhaps you identify most with this group. You may not feel you are an initiator, but you always move quickly to show support and to secure the ground the activists are taking. This is a vital role when it comes to reaching across the divide. Re-activists are good people to have over for dinner on that first occasion when someone takes the plunge and invites people from another culture for a meal. The host knows with confidence that their re-activist friend will be only too willing to help build relationships across the divide and support the process of change. If you are a re-activist, you may already be asking yourself which initiatives you might be able to get behind and which people are likely to be active in initiating change. Beware; you may just find God is asking you to become one of the initiators yourself! Here are three things you can do as a re-activist:

- **Pray** that God will give you opportunities to support others as they attempt to build relationships across the divide. Your role may also be key in ensuring that activists don't run too far ahead and that passive supporters don't lag too far behind.
- **Read** parts of this book again. (On the second occasion you'll find fewer surprises, but you might gain greater clarity on how God wants you to respond in your own context.)

- **Reach out:** Be an encourager to other people as they progress on their journey. In that first diverse church leadership team which we find in Acts 13, we read of Barnabas, who was known as the 'son of encouragement'. People and churches that make progress on this issue need lots of help, support and encouragement from people like you.

One person's journey

My wife Pauline is a re-activist. She says of herself that she would never have sought change, or reached out to people from other cultures on her own in the way that we have been able to do together. Even in the way we do hospitality, she has moved, changed and adapted. I have learnt more from her about the white British culture than from any other person I know. Without her, I could not reach across the divides in the way that I do.

Pauline was born in south east London and grew up in Kent, moving back to London when we got married. When I first met her over twenty years ago, she was not even a passive supporter of diversity. She was not anti, either; she was just unaware. This is not surprising really, as she grew up in an environment where, before meeting me, she could have counted on the fingers of one hand the number of people she had met who were different from her (and still have fingers left to spare!). Pauline found it difficult to believe that diversity made any difference at all. She couldn't believe that people were still judged by their accent or skin colour, or any other difference you care to name. During the years of friendship and dating, we lived very much in a world of things in common: faith, friends and fun could have summed up our experience. Differences were minimal because we didn't focus on them.

Differences in marriage

Once we married, differences began to surface: not just the usual differences which any couple has to grapple with, but cultural ones. A little example came while planning our wedding. From my background, wedding speeches were not limited to the best man and the father of the bride. Anyone who wanted to give a blessing or bring some words of encouragement to the newly married couple was free to do so. Pauline's family couldn't quite understand why people did that, and were concerned about the time it might take. In my experience, they were right to be concerned, as these speeches could go on for some time! Nevertheless, we made space for them, because it was a strong part of the culture, and people valued the opportunity to say their piece.

Other differences occurred in areas like our family traditions and expectations, and in our attitudes to things like money and the world around us, based on our histories and experiences. Suddenly, we were grappling with the reality of difference in our everyday lives. Tensions arose from being different and from not fully understanding or appreciating those differences. For example, I grew up in an environment where I observed my parents regularly supporting family in Jamaica. This meant sending money and visiting, and taking numerous gifts for family and friends. This was clearly an expectation within the culture. Pauline grew up in an environment where there was no such expectation; indeed the opposite expectation was in place, because her grandparents supported her parents. As we and our parents have got older we live with both expectations.

Being married has meant that we have had no choice but to face these issues and work through them. Our relationship has always been more important to us than any one issue we face. Walking away has never been an option. Yet, despite the occasional tense moments, we have found a depth and a richness in our relationship as we have explored each other's backgrounds and cultures. Openness, acceptance and honesty probably best sum up our relationship. Nowadays, listening to an English girl from Kent trying to speak *patois* (a Jamaican Creole language) brings much laughter in our house! We always try to model to our three girls a lifestyle of inclusive living. All people matter to God regardless of background, and therefore they matter to us.

The church should be 'married'

In many ways, our marriage mirrors the church on this issue. God has brought people together to display something of who he is. In a sense, we, the church, are married to one another. In the Bible, metaphors for the church include a bride (Revelation 19:7), a body (1 Corinthians 12:12) and a family (Galatians 6:10), all speaking of diversity, unity and togetherness. As people of diversity come together, we love to celebrate and enjoy the things we have in common. Our worship and love of Jesus is the primary example of that. As in a love relationship, enjoyment of one another's food and celebrations often rank fairly high! But equally, as can happen in a marriage, our differences begin to emerge. At this point, we must realize that we are 'married' to one another, united in this relationship and joined as one. God calls us to be together, not to separate or withdraw at the first sign of trouble or difficulty. As we continue together, like a married couple we learn to appreciate our differences and grow closer together. That is certainly my experience in marriage.

Bridge-builders

A bridge-builder is someone who becomes familiar with the ways of another culture as well as their own. They can 'speak the language': that is, communicate in a way that enables them to be heard and understood. Not only this, but they are respected in more than one culture. Also, importantly, a bridge-builder is comfortable in more than one culture. I want to look at one Old Testament character who was a prime example of a bridge-builder: Moses. What can we learn from him?

Moses the bridge-builder

'By faith Moses, when he had grown up, refused to be known as the son of Pharaoh's daughter. He chose to be ill-treated along with the people of God' (Hebrews 11:24).

Having been brought up as a member of the royal household, Moses was both entitled to and expected to take on a royal identity. However, he chose to forgo the comforts and privileges that came with being a member of the royal line of Egypt, and instead chose to be identified with the people of God, Israel. Even while living as an Egyptian, his heart was in Israel. He killed an Egyptian he saw attacking an Israelite and attempted to be a peacemaker between two Israelites fighting. Moses was making his own attempts to build bridges and failing miserably. After he realized his crime had been discovered by both the Israelites and Pharaoh, he fled from Egypt and wandered in the desert, where he became a shepherd for forty years.

The Egyptian Israelite

But Moses was God's chosen instrument to take the people out of Egypt. Why Moses? There may be a number of reasons, but let me give you just one. Moses was a bridge-builder. You could have called him the Egyptian Israelite. He would have looked and sounded like an Egyptian (Exodus 2:19), understanding their language, ways and culture, but in his heart he was an Israelite. He was part of the people of

God. He was in the perfect position to stand before Pharaoh. He was also in the perfect position to lead the people of Israel out of Egypt, because he was an Israelite and identified himself as one of them. God chose Moses, partly because he understood both cultures.

Some modern-day examples

Some people have described Joel Edwards, former General Director of the Evangelical Alliance, as a bridge-builder. He certainly built many bridges: across racial divides, a wide and varied spectrum of evangelical groups, and, importantly, with the culture around us. I know many bridge-builders. Whether it is building bridges to young people, poor people, rich people, unbelieving people, deaf people, disabled people, or people from different races and cultures, the world needs more bridge-builders who can help link people across the divide.

Jesus the ultimate bridge-builder

Jesus was the ultimate bridge-builder. He left his Father's throne to reach across the chasm and the great divide of sin, and bring us into a relationship with God. Crossing the divide is what life in him is all about. Jesus did it and we are called to do the same.

A parallel example

'Diversity is more complex than I first realized,' says Steve Tibbert of King's Church. 'The closest thing to what we are currently experiencing is renewal, when the church needed to change its wineskin for new wine.'

Restoring the church

Thirty to forty years ago, God began a particular work of restoration in his church in the UK. People who were longing for a fresh and deeper experience of God were being filled with the Holy Spirit. A fresh understanding of local church life, and of the role of the foundational ministries of apostles, prophets, evangelist, pastors and teachers, was breaking out. What was required was a new wineskin, as the old structures of church were not necessarily going to be sufficient to hold this new wine. Many of us reading this book are reaping the blessings which have come as a result of those early days of restoration. Often we embrace these blessings without question. We can't imagine church life without the vibrancy we now enjoy, and we can't imagine life without the Holy Spirit bringing new and fresh things to our lives.

Early pioneers

That was not the experience of many of the early pioneers of that movement of the Spirit. Terry Virgo, the founding father of the Newfrontiers Movement that I have had the privilege of being a part of for the last thirty years, along with many others, grappled and battled with these issues. He searched the Scriptures and wrestled with God and found emphatically God's plan and purpose for the local church. It wasn't that one or two Scriptures could be made to fit a new and fresh experience, but a realization that this had always been God's plan. The acceptance of the work of apostles, prophets and church planting in mission is now evident in the wider church body. For years, Christians expressed these new values in small groups, local churches and in special Bible weeks.

Let's go

A few years ago, God spoke to the leaders of the Newfrontiers family of churches, telling them that the time had come to close the highly influential Stoneleigh Bible Week, and instead support and encourage churches to focus on mission. 'Let's Go' became the mandate for change. As a family of churches, we went back into our villages, towns and cities, planting churches and sharing Jesus wherever we went. For many of us, the world we met was different from what we might ever have expected. As we met real people, they weren't all just like us. Many looked different, spoke differently, and had completely different values and beliefs. One of the elders at my home church, a pastor for many years, said he has experienced a greater variety of pastoral issues in the last few years than in all the previous years he has been in ministry.

The danger of the old wineskin

One of the biggest dangers is that we merely attempt to squeeze our increasingly diverse churches into an existing and possibly fairly monocultural mindset. Keeping the Bible as our guide, we will need to examine the way we do things. We may discover that some of our deeply held values and organizational practices are more cultural than we realized. Issues we may have to look at are: how and when we pray, how we meet in small groups, the place of children in the church, how we train people, and how we worship together. Offering debt, marriage and parenting courses might become a more regular feature of church life.

Implications of diversity

For the city

The world around us has become more secular in attitude, but more hungry for spiritual things. Increasingly our churches are not made up of people who look, sound or think like us. What we once only experienced on the mission fields of India, South America and Africa we now experience in London, Newcastle and Brighton. London, in particular, is a city into which the world has come: its influence goes far beyond its small geographical sphere. God calls his church to reach the city and embrace the diversity within it, and in so doing to touch the world.

For mission

This has radical implications for the way we view mission. In the past, many have travelled to other nations for mission, to reach various people groups. Often these trips have been fruitful, but tough and slow going. However, a new world mission opportunity has arisen. We can now reach the nations of the world by reaching the people who live next door. While some have settled here, many desire to return to their home nation. I once had a man approach me at my church and say, 'I want to plant a church like this in my home nation.' We have the opportunity to reach them with the gospel of Christ, envisioning, training and equipping them, before sending them back to their nations with a heart to plant local churches and reach their nations for Jesus.

John Kpikpi, who leads a growing, thriving church in Accra, Ghana, is an example of someone who was saved, envisioned and equipped in the UK before returning to his home nation. Now he leads a church and is planting other churches. In 2007, I visited Metropolitan Tabernacle in London. I was amazed when I read a church brochure and saw the number of people they had sent back to their original nations to lead churches and ministries there.

For us

The whole purpose of this book is to help churches that are just beginning to embrace diversity to understand more of the issues they are facing and the huge potential of embracing all God has for us. God will not force his purpose upon us, nor make us embrace diversity. He waits for a generation ready and willing to embrace his purposes, whatever the cost. My prayer, like the prayers of many others who have pioneered and seen ahead, is that this generation will be the one that embraces all God is doing in the earth today, and sees the significance of diversity in unity, for the glory of God.

Questions for discussion

Where can you start to cross the divide in relationships?

Are you a passive, activist or re-activist supporter of diversity?

In what ways or areas can you build bridges to people not like you?

Complete the questionnaire in the Appendix and discuss your findings with someone you know well.

APPENDIX: QUESTIONNAIRE ON DIVERSITY AWARENESS

1. What percentage of the church you attend would you describe as coming from a different background from yourself?
2. Has the church you attend grown in diversity over the last few years? If so, what type of diversity?
3. How many of these diverse people do you know, and in what capacity do you know them?
4. How many of your personal friendships are with people from a background different from your own, and do you ever discuss your differences?
5. Have you ever been discriminated against because you were different?
6. Do you spend time with people outside your own group? How does this influence your perception of other groups?
7. Do you harbour any negative feelings of resentment towards people of another group? If so, why do you

think this is? What would help you deal with those feelings?

8. Do you hold any negative stereotypes toward people of another group? If so, why do you think this is? What can you do to change those stereotypes?

9. In what ways could you increase your own awareness and understanding of diversity? Would this help you to cross the divide more often?

FURTHER READING

The reader will gain further information and enlightenment in connection with the issues raised in this book from the following works:

David A. Anderson, *Gracism: The Art of Inclusion*, InterVarsity Press, 2007

David A. Anderson, *Multicultural Ministry: Finding your Church's Unique Rhythm*, Zondervan, 2004

David A. Anderson and Brent Zuercher, *Letters Across the Divide: Two Friends Explore Racism, Friendship, and Faith*, Baker Books, 2001

Curtiss Paul DeYoung, Michael O. Emerson, George Yancey and Karen Chai Kim, *United by Faith: The Multiracial Congregation as an Answer to the Problem of Race*, Oxford University Press, 2003

Michael O. Emerson, *People of the Dream: Multiracial Congregations in the United States*, Princeton University Press, 2006

Michael O. Emerson and Christian Smith, *Divided by Faith: Evangelical Religion and the Problem of Race in America*, Oxford University Press, USA, 2001

J. Daniel Hays, *From Every People and Nation: A Biblical Theology of Race*, Inter-Varsity Press, 2003

David Killingray and Joel Edwards, *Black Voices: The Shaping of Our Christian Experience*, Inter-Varsity Press, 2007

John Kpikpi, *God's New Tribe*, Hill City Publishing, 2003

Bruce Milne, *Dynamic Diversity: The New Humanity Church for Today and Tomorrow*, Inter-Varsity Press, 2006

Terry Muck (General Editor), *NIV Application Commentary Series*, various volumes, Zondervan

Trevor Phillips and Mike Phillips, *Windrush: The Irresistible Rise of Multi-Racial Britain*, Harper Collins Publishers, 1999

John Piper, *Let the Nations be Glad: The Supremacy of God in Missions*, Inter-Varsity Press/Baker Academic, 2003

Linbert Spencer, *Building a Multi-ethnic Church*, SPCK, 2007

Mark Sturge, *Look What the Lord Has Done! An Exploration of Black Christian Faith in Britain*, Scripture Union Publishing, 2005

Derek Tidball, *The Message of the Cross*, The Bible Speaks Today series, Inter-Varsity Press, 2003

Desmond Tutu, *No Future Without Forgiveness*, Rider, 1999

George Yancey, *One Body, One Spirit: Principles of Successful Multiracial Churches*, InterVarsity Press, 2001

NOTES

Introduction
King's Church, Catford: www.kingscentre.org.uk.

Beacon Church, south central London: www.beaconchurchlondon.
org.uk.

David A. Anderson, *Gracism: The Art of Inclusion*, InterVarsity Press,
2007, p. 11.

John Piper, *Let the Nations be Glad: The Supremacy of God in Missions*,
Inter-Varsity Press Baker/Academic, 2003, p. 198.

Chapter 1 Why is the issue of diversity so important to the church today?
Statistics from 'Born Abroad: an immigration map of Britain' based
on research carried out by the Institute for Public Policy Research,
www.bbc.co.uk/bornabroad, 7 September 2005.

Statistics taken from English Church Census 2005 in *Religious Trends
6* and *Pulling out of the Nosedive*, Christian Research 2006:
www.christian-research.org.uk.

David A. Anderson, *Gracism: The Art of Inclusion*, InterVarsity Press,
2007, p. 41.

John R. W. Stott, *The Message of Ephesians*, The Bible Speaks Today
series, Inter-Varsity Press, 1979, p. 111.

Some of the ideas in this chapter were suggested or clarified by:

J. Daniel Hays, *From Every People and Nation: A Biblical Theology of
Race*, Inter-Varsity Press, 2003.

Chapter 2 'I thought we were all the same, so what's the issue?'

Douglas Adams, *A Hitchhiker's Guide to the Galaxy*, Pan Macmillan, 1979.

The Apprentice, series four, TV programme produced by talkbackTHAMES for the BBC, March 2008.

Stephen B. Oates, *Let The Trumpet Sound: A Life Of Martin Luther King*, HarperPerennial, 1994, p. 372.

Chapter 3 What about other forms of diversity? Why focus on racial diversity?

Deaflympics: www.deaflympics.com.

Evangelical Alliance: www.eauk.org.

Micah Challenge: www.micahchallenge.org.uk.

Alpha UK: www.uk.alpha.org.

Newfrontiers: www.newfrontiers.xtn.org.

Mars Hill Church: www.marshillchurch.org.

Alexander Solzhenitsyn, *The Gulag Archipelago*, cited in Nicky Gumbel, *Questions of Life: An Opportunity to Explore the Meaning of Life*, Kingsway, 2001, p. 18.

David A. Anderson, *Multicultural Ministry: Finding your Church's Unique Rhythm*, Zondervan, 2004.

Some of the ideas in this chapter were suggested or clarified by:

Gary Chapman, *The Five Love Languages for Singles*, Northfield Publishing USA, 2004.

Bruce Milne, *Dynamic Diversity: The New Humanity Church for Today and Tomorrow*, Inter-Varsity Press, 2006.

Chapter 4 What about history and issues of legacy?

Kingdom of Heaven, film directed by Ridley Scott, 2005.

Racism in America comments by D. A. Carson, interview at Southern Baptist Theological Seminary, 2004.

Jane Elliott: www.janeelliott.com.

Senator Barack Obama, 'A More Perfect Union' speech, Philadelphia, USA, 18 March 2008.

R. T. Kendall, *The Parables of Jesus: A Guide to Understanding and Applying the Stories of Jesus*, Sovereign World, 2006.

Bishop John Francis, quoted in *Charisma* magazine, Strang Communications, June 2000.

Chapter 5 What about issues of forgiveness, repentance and reconciliation?

Corrie ten Boom, *The Hiding Place*, quoted in 'I'm Still Learning to Forgive', Good News Publishers, 1995, reprinted by permission from *Guideposts* magazine, Guideposts Associates, Inc., Carmel, New York 10512, 1972.

John D. Roth, cited in David E. Garland, *NIV Application Commentary: Colossians/Philemon*, Zondervan, 1998, p. 309.

Desmond Tutu, *No Future Without Forgiveness*, Rider, 1999, p. 121.

Chapter 6 Why should we cross the divide in relationships and what are the benefits?

John Piper, sermon on Ephesians 2, Bethlehem Baptist Church, Minneapolis, Minnesota, USA, 2000: www.desiringgodministries.com.

Bruce Milne, *Dynamic Diversity: The New Humanity Church for Today and Tomorrow*, Inter-Varsity Press, 2006, p. 22.

Derek Tidball, *The Message of the Cross*, The Bible Speaks Today series, Inter-Varsity Press, 2001, p. 226.

Chapter 7 How do I develop relationships across the divide?

The Lord of the Rings trilogy: *The Fellowship of the Ring*, film directed by Peter Jackson, 2001.

Bruce Milne, *Dynamic Diversity: The New Humanity Church for Today and Tomorrow*, Inter-Varsity Press, 2006.

Some of the ideas in this chapter were suggested or clarified by:
Curtiss Paul DeYoung, Michael O. Emerson, George Yancey and
    Karen Chai Kim, *United by Faith: The Multiracial Congregation as an
    Answer to the Problem of Race*, OUP, 2003.

Chapter 8 How do we integrate people from different backgrounds into church life?

Tim King, 'A French Brixton', *Prospect* magazine, December 2005.
Antioch church model: Curtiss Paul DeYoung et al, *United by Faith:
    The Multiracial Congregation as an Answer to the Problem of Race*,
    OUP, 2003, p. 28.
Shelly Collins, Diversity Awareness Training, King's Church,
    Catford.

Chapter 9 What does a truly diverse church look like?

Quotation from Dr James Forbes, from Curtiss Paul DeYoung et
    al, *United by Faith: The Multiracial Congregation as an Answer to the
    Problem of Race*, OUP, 2003, p. 82.
Bruce Milne, *Dynamic Diversity: The New Humanity Church for Today
    and Tomorrow*, Inter-Varsity Press, 2006, p. 168.
George Yancey, *One Body, One Spirit: Principles of Successful
    Multiracial Churches*, Inter-Varsity Press, 2001, p. 15.
'In Christ alone my hope is found', words and music by Stuart
    Townend and Keith Getty, Kingsway, 2002.
Some of the ideas in this chapter were suggested or clarified by:
Linbert Spencer, *Building a Multi-ethnic Church*, SPCK, 2007.

Chapter 10 'I want to cross the race divide, so where do I start?'

Cry Freedom, film directed by Richard Attenborough, 1987.

Related titles from

Bruce Milne

DYNAMIC DIVERSITY

The new humanity church for today and tomorrow

A single new community, embracing all diversity, is God's idea for his church.

From the footpaths of our cities to the chat rooms of the Internet, people are connecting today as never before.

In this context of in-your-face diversity, it is time to revisit the heart of the New Testament, with its claim that in Jesus Christ a new quality of human relationship is possible. In his letter to the Ephesians, the apostle Paul claims that Christians are a new kind of people, part of a new community: a 'new humanity' in Christ (Ephesians 2:15). We exist not in isolation, but in relationship.

Dynamic Diversity contends that all Christian congregations everywhere are called to be bridging places, centres of reconciliation, where the major diversities separating human beings are overcome through the presence of God's Holy Spirit. In Christ we can be one people, one new humanity, one life.

'This is an invaluable, scholarly and accessible tool for all leaders and thinking Christians who want to grapple with the challenges and privileges of holding unity in diversity.'
Joel Edwards

ISBN:
978-1-84474-158-8

Available from your local Christian bookshop or via our website at **www.ivpbooks.com**

www.ivpbooks.com

For more details of books published by IVP, visit our website where you will find all the latest information, including:

Book extracts   Downloads
Author interviews   Online bookshop
Reviews   Christian bookshop finder

You can also sign up for our regular email newsletters, which are tailored to your particular interests, and tell others what you think about this book by posting a review.

We publish a wide range of books on various subjects including:

Christian living   Small-group resources
Key reference works   Topical issues
Bible commentary series Theological studies